THE IDEAL CITY

EDITED WITH AN INTRODUCTION BY
HELEN E. MELLER

The Ideal City
by Canon Barnett
&
Civics: as Applied Sociology
by Patrick Geddes

LEICESTER UNIVERSITY PRESS
1979

The Ideal City by Canon Barnett
first published about 1893–4
Civics: as Applied Sociology by Patrick Geddes
first published in 1905–6

Victorian Library edition published in 1979 by
Leicester University Press

Distributed in North America by
Humanities Press Inc., New Jersey

Introduction copyright © Leicester University Press 1979
Printed in Great Britain by
Unwin Brothers Limited
The Gresham Press, Old Woking, Surrey
A member of the Staples Printing Group

ISBN 0 7185 5034 X (paperback)
ISBN 0 7185 5061 (cased)

THE VICTORIAN LIBRARY

2

THE IDEAL CITY

THE VICTORIAN LIBRARY

It is the object of this series to make available again a selection of classic works of Victorian literature in several fields. Most of the volumes are reprinted photographically from the first edition or another chosen because it has some special value, so that an accurate text is ensured. Others, of which this volume is an example, contain a selection of Victorian writings focused on a specific theme. Each volume carries a substantial introduction by an authority on the author or the subject, and gives bibliographical details.

Recommendation of titles for THE VICTORIAN LIBRARY and of scholars to contribute the Introductions is made by a joint committee of the Board of the University Press and the Victorian Studies Centre of the University of Leicester.

Titles published include the following

Vestiges of the Natural History of Creation
Robert Chambers   Introduction by Sir Gavin de Beer

Autobiography and Deliverance
Mark Rutherford   Introduction by Basil Willey

Contrasts
A. W. N. Pugin   Introduction by H. R. Hitchcock

The Medical and Legal Aspects of Sanitary Reform
A. P. Stewart and E. Jenkins   Introduction by M. W. Flinn

A Discourse on the Studies of the University
Adam Sedgwick   Introduction by Sir Eric Ashby and Mary Anderson

Chartism
William Lovett   Introduction by Asa Briggs

The Bitter Cry of Outcast London
Andrew Mearns   With leading articles from the *Pall Mall Gazette* of October 1883 and articles by Lord Salisbury, Joseph Chamberlain and Forster Crozier   Edited with an introduction by Anthony S. Wohl

Phases of Faith
F. W. Newman   Introduction by U. C. Knoepflmacher

Murray's Handbook for Travellers in Switzerland 1838
Introduction by Jack Simmons

Midlothian Speeches 1879
W. E. Gladstone   Introduction by M. R. D. Foot

Twice Round the Clock
George Augustus Sala   Introduction by Philip Collins

The Great Landowners of Great Britain and Ireland
John Bateman   Introduction by David Spring

Movements of Religious Thought in Britain during the Nineteenth Century
John Tulloch   Introduction by A. C. Cheyne

The Life of Thomas Cooper
Thomas Cooper   Introduction by John Saville

Town Swamps and Social Bridges
George Godwin   Introduction by Anthony D. King

School Architecture
E. R. Robson   With additional plates, bibliography, and list of Robson's educational buildings   Introduction by Malcolm Seaborne

Oakfield: or Fellowship in the East
W. D. Arnold   Introduction by Kenneth Allott

Collins' Illustrated Atlas of London
Introduction by H. J. Dyos

Autobiography and Letters of Mrs Margaret Oliphant
Edited by Mrs Harry Coghill   Introduction, and notes on persons mentioned in the text, by Q. D. Leavis

Journal of a London Playgoer
Henry Morley   Introduction by Michael R. Booth

The New Republic
W. H. Mallock   Introduction by John Lucas

Children of the Ghetto
Israel Zangwill   Introduction by V. D. Lipman

A History of the Gothic Revival
Charles L. Eastlake   With corrected appendix, additional illustrations, bibliography and index.   Edited with an introduction by J. Mordaunt Crook

Images of Race
Edited with an introduction by Michael D. Biddiss

Educating our Masters
Edited with an introduction by David Reeder

CONTENTS

INTRODUCTION

Canon Barnett and Sir Patrick Geddes have had an influence on
modern responses to city life which has far transcended the impact
made by their published work alone. Both were men of action.
However, it was action mingled with theory. They shared a commitment to a conception of evolutionary social theory in which
social progress, their common objective, came through a combination
of individual action and informed theory. The search for such a
social theory was undertaken, not in the study, but in society at
large, and ideas were translated into organized voluntary activities
which were regarded as controlled 'scientific' experiments. It was
this attempt to provide a sociological basis for practical work, in
as 'scientific' a manner as possible, which unites the work of Barnett
and Geddes, and makes it interesting and informative to compare
and contrast their methods and results. Theirs was a rare contribution. They sought to understand the implications of the twin
processes of urbanization and industrialization, not in terms of any
abstract theory, but in the context of a specific environment,
starting from the experiences of individuals and families. The most
formidable task that they both shared was thus, to comprehend the
modern industrial and commercial city, in its totality, from the
viewpoint of those living in it.

The papers reprinted here, Barnett's *The Ideal City* and Geddes's
two papers on 'Civics: as applied sociology' give, in a succinct form,
the fruits of their labours. The very nature of their work, action
informing theory, and theory action, precluded the possibility that
either would write a sociological monograph outlining and explaining
their work. Both, however, published prolifically, mainly in the
form of magazine articles, occasional pamphlets and reviews. A
select list of Barnett's writings appears at the end of volume two

of his wife's biography *Canon Barnett, his life, work and friends*
(1918) and an almost complete list of Geddes's writings is published
as Appendice A in P. Boardman's *Esquisse de L'oeuvre educatrice
de Patrick Geddes* (Montpellier, 1936).

There are two volumes though, which should be used as supple-
ments to the articles reprinted here. All the ideas contained in
Barnett's *Ideal City* are to be found in a number of articles Barnett
wrote, which he and his wife (who added some articles of her own)
collected together into one volume, *Practicable Socialism: essays
in social reform* (1888). The key articles, first published in *The
Nineteenth Century*, are: 'Practicable Socialism' (1883), 'Town
Councils and Social Reform' (1883) and 'University Settlements'
(1884). The volume which should be consulted to supplement Geddes'
papers, is his report on Dunfermline, *City Development: A Study
of Parks, Gardens, and Culture-Institutes* (Edinburgh and Bourn-
ville, 1904). He wrote it as a result of his first commission to put
his ideas into practice, and he himself used the volume as a practical
illustration of his theory of civics, as outlined in his papers, 'Civics:
as applied sociology'.

During their lifetimes, Barnett and Geddes were both hailed as
prophets,[1] and they were given the status of founding fathers in
two important new disciplines, scientific social administration and
town planning. Yet characteristically, it was their approach to the
social problems of cities which was admired, rather than their ideas.
Many contemporaries have stated how much they owed to the
stimulus Barnett and Geddes provided,[2] but subsequent generations
have been puzzled as to why they were once so influential. The
answer does not lie in their written work, though this is all we
have. It is easy with hindsight, to pinpoint the limitations of their
thought and action.[3] But this is not really the point. What they
were trying to do, in the words of the Charity Organisation Society
Annual Report of 1902–3, was to induce people ' "to think" and not
to shrink from applying theory to practical work'. They were
concerned not so much with working out a system of thought as
with trying to establish a new outlook, a more effective way of
looking at social conditions. Their 'thinking' had a double objective:
to provide a range of concepts to make city life readily intelligible,
and to promote informed social action.

Both the papers reprinted here are optimistic in tone. By a coincidence, they were written when both men were nearing 50 years of age. Barnett (1844–1913) wrote *The Ideal City* shortly after being appointed to a Canonry of Bristol Cathedral in 1893, after 20 years of work in the East End of London as vicar of St Judes, Whitechapel, and after ten years as Warden of Toynbee Hall, the University settlement. The latter was his most important practical achievement and he was to remain as Warden until 1906. Geddes (1854–1932) presented his two papers in 1904 and 1905, at the first and second sessions of the newly founded British Sociological Society. He had recently decided to make London his centre of activities after 20 years work in Edinburgh, the last ten of which had seen the creation and development of the Outlook Tower, his civic and regional museum, with all its attendant activities. This was to be his most important practical achievement in Britain. Yet both men suffered many disappointments in their work, and in their old age both, on occasions, gave way to despondency.[4]

Their earlier optimism had been based on a confidence that they had found the key to improve the social condition of cities. What differentiates them from other social reformers and philanthropists was their concern, not with specific social problems, but with the whole context of social life in the city. What they wanted was to establish better norms for urban living. They believed that deep-seated social problems could only be solved in a new climate of understanding about cities and their influence on people. Thus for Barnett the key was social relationships. If only people got to know one another, especially people from different classes now segregated by the economic forces of modern urban growth, then the necessary concern and knowledge to overcome all problems could be found. For Geddes, the key was a better understanding of the city and its region. Whilst other observers became crushed by the complexities of city life and the interaction of different factors on the well-being of individuals, Geddes offered a geographical and historical approach. He placed the city firmly in its region, providing at one and the same time, a rural/urban perspective on city life, and a highly idiosyncratic method of analysing occupations and social structure which, at least, gave a promise of insight into city life to those urgently seeking to understand it.

In the 1880s and 1890s there was a groundswell of demand for
new insight which drew people to Barnett and Geddes and their
practical activities. Both men were thus led to believe that their
ideas could be communicated and given form through the action of
voluntary workers. To inspire such work however, and to infuse it
with moral purpose, Barnett and Geddes had recourse to the all-
purpose concept of citizenship, which they imbued with special
meaning. In *The Ideal City* and 'Civics: as applied Sociology', better
citizenship is the road to social progress. Both men were deeply
influenced by the nineteenth-century concept of community and for
both, community spirit was equated with citizenship.[5] Voluntary
action by private individuals for the public good within the framework of the local community of a city, was what they sought. The
benefit to the voluntary worker was both emotional and intellectual.
Doing good and helping the poor brought emotional satisfaction.
Intellectually, the voluntary worker would have a new insight into
modern society. The core of Barnett's message to his followers was:
'know your local community and you can understand society', to
which Geddes added: 'know your region and you can understand the
world'.

Utopia – ideal or reality?

The main significance of *The Ideal City* and 'Civics: as applied
sociology' does not however, lie simply in this message. Both authors
were even more concerned with the implications of their approach,
and practical ways of achieving social progress. The next two
sections of this introduction will be devoted to these aspects. Barnett
and Geddes only put their ideas on paper to stimulate the kind of
action they wanted and they always gave more weight to the
practical outcome of their work than to their own position as social
philosophers. As has already been pointed out, the ideas in these
papers were not new to their authors when they were written. What
is significant is that they were produced after both men had had a
number of successes in their practical work.

By 1893, Barnett had contributed much to a transformation of
the parish of St Judes. There had been extensive slum clearance, the
building of blocks of improved dwellings and a marked improvement
in social institutions in the parish, particularly those of an educational and recreational nature. By 1904, Geddes had not only had

considerable successes with his Edinburgh improvements, his Outlook Tower and Edinburgh Summer Meetings; he had also gained
an international reputation by holding his yearly summer meeting
in 1900 at Paris, at the World International Exposition.[6] His
International Summer School, designed to provide a guide to an
understanding of the contemporary world, was backed by an organization, the International Association for the Advancement of the
Sciences, Art and Education, which he had set up, though it proved
short-lived as he ran out of money after the International Exibition
in Glasgow the following year. What Barnett and Geddes were doing
in these papers was thus giving the fruits of their experiences rather
than merely outlining their social philosophies.

The major implications of this were that both wanted to inspire
action and for this purpose both had recourse to a visionary idealism
or utopianism. What they both wanted to prove however, by their
own example, was that their vision of Utopia was no day-dream.
It was what could be achieved by informed social action. They were
'practical' idealists, a distinction they insisted on to differentiate
themselves from the philosophical Idealists and the Utopians. Barnett, a student at Oxford, had become acquainted with the philosophical idealism of T. H. Green and his circle, who were concerned
with creating a new moral order to be made manifest, in a practical
way, by enlightened citizenship.[7] But Barnett's idealism, though it
was nurtured in this environment, was more precisely concentrated
on actual ways of achieving social reform. For him, the 'ideal' was
what could be realized by those with the will-power and moral
purpose to do it. The 'ideal' provided the social reformer with the
necessary 'vision', to sustain him in his work.

As for Utopia and Geddes, he always drew a sharp contrast
between himself and others, like Ebenezer Howard, even when
Howard's Utopia came into being with the foundation of the Garden
City Company and the development of Letchworth. Utopia for
Geddes was not an experiment outside the economic and social
conditions of modern society.[8] His Utopia was Eutopia, what could
be achieved, given those economics and social factors, to create a
higher civilization. His Eutopia was, in fact, the opposite of Utopia
which, by definition, was never to be attained. Why Geddes and
Barnett used this method of providing an ideal which all could

aspire to, since it was realizable, and why a significant number were to be inspired by their vision, is a question which can only be answered in the broad context of time, place and character. For all their emphasis on the needs of the future which made them both appear to be progressive, even ahead of their time, their concern and the responses they received were firmly rooted in the events and experiences of late Victorian, early Edwardian Britain. Their attraction was that they offered, largely it is true to an educated middle-class elite, the chance to undertake practical work in the city which went beyond the confines of philanthropic work or local government at that time. Their use of 'idealism' has to be set in the context of contemporary concern over the social implications of mass urbanization.

Dissatisfaction with the conventional responses to urban problems had, by the 1870s and 1880s, become widespread. In the last quarter of the nineteenth century many of the facts of urban life had been more systematically revealed. Royal Commissions had studied such sensitive subjects as the sanitary condition of large cities since the 1848 Act, the housing of the working classes, the treatment of the aged poor, and the progress of elementary and secondary education. In the 1880s, the press and pamphlet literature exploited the more sensational aspects of city life, the vice and crime; whilst Charles Booth had undertaken the fullest, most objective and accurate survey of London ever taken, which revealed that 30 per cent of London's citizens lived in poverty, ten per cent of whom had an income below subsistence level. Knowledge of the 'submerged tenth' was the final revelation to destroy the complacency of the ruling classes.[9] It was becoming obvious that economic progress had not led to social progress and the growing problems of the large cities were there to prove it.

Barnett's and Geddes's use of idealism sprang from their desire to alter the course of events so that social progress could be achieved in the future. They tried to provide for themselves a conception of past, present and future which would preserve the idea of progress. The framework of past, present and future constructed by the masters of political economy which had sustained earlier generations had suddenly, in the 1860s and 1870s, seemed less solid. Leading economists themselves, like W. S. Jevons, began to think in terms not of unlimited economic progress but in the predictable limitations of resources, and he in his spare time, concerned himself with social reform.[10] The young Alfred Marshall found his vocation for the 'dismal science' by walking the streets in the poor areas of large towns and looking at the faces he saw. He felt a moral obligation to find out why such social conditions existed.[11]

Faith that political economy could provide the answers, however, was not widespread.[12] There was a burgeoning of studies in areas newly defined as the social sciences, which in America, France and Germany resulted in the establishment of new institutions and disciplines. In Britain, the academic establishment was slower to respond. Even the natural sciences, in which British scientists such as Darwin and Wallace had made such outstanding contributions, were barely given adequate support. Britain's leading educationalist in the natural sciences, T. H. Huxley, spent much of his early career giving concentrated short courses to improve the general knowledge of student engineers at London's Royal School of Mines.[13] Yet on an amateur basis, there was a movement towards the social sciences, especially sociology, in Britain in the 1870s which caught up many others besides Barnett and Geddes.

At this time Herbert Spencer was at the peak of his influence in Britain. But disillusionment was to be the only reward of the earnest seekers after truth who turned to him, as Spencer believed that the role of the sociologist was to observe, not to act. No individual, in his opinion, could hope to counter the great evolutionary forces shaping man and his society.[14] For those, like Barnett and Geddes, whose desire to act was much stronger than their academic interest in society, he provided no guidance. They had to struggle, and disagree amongst themselves on how to measure social progress and how to influence its future direction. Geddes turned to the French sociological school of Le Play for his guidance; Barnett towards the innovatory traditions of English philanthropy. Yet both were determined to answer the problems posed by sociologists on the nature and direction of social progress, and both wanted to orientate their studies towards providing guidelines for practical work.

In the mid-1870s, Geddes was serving his apprenticeship for the future, a young Scottish student in London, studying the implications of evolutionary theory in the natural sciences under T. H.

Huxley at the Royal School of Mines; and tramping the streets of
London, then the greatest city in the world, in his spare time.
London was not only a capital city and the largest port, it was also
the centre of a growing world multilateral economic system in which
the development of resources and opening up of virgin territories
were creating closer economic links between all nations. London's
financiers and brokers, merchants and insurance underwriters, provided the expertise, impetus and services which kept the system in
operation and engineered the fastest increase ever in world productive capacity. The wealth of the city was unparalleled, yet alongside
the ostentatious display of power and riches were the areas of great
poverty and suffering, where all the urban problems became mag-
nified by their concentration.[15]

Geddes's views on the evils of the economic system and the
degradation of humanity which had resulted from the unharnessed
exploitation of modern technology, were formed here. Much of his
later a-political stance stemmed from the belief that this had
happened because people had become mesmerized by the very
machines they had created, and disputes about who should own
what, or how the results of new wealth should be shared out, were
irrelevant. What was needed was to break out of the intellectual
mould imposed by industrialization, and instead, create a new way
of thinking centred on the production and development, not of
goods, but of people. For him, this was a biological viewpoint, a
matter of common sense, which could be achieved through a height-
ened level of public morality. It had little to do with politics, with
the world of high finance or the factory system.[16] He gave a series
of lectures to the Royal Institution in Edinburgh and other bodies
in the 1880s which elaborated on this theme.[17]

In 1873, Barnett was appointed to his first post as a Church of
England clergyman in the slum parish of St Judes in the East End.
His wife tells of the heart-searching which went on before the
decision to take the post was made. With his connections and
promise, Barnett might have found a parish with a rich and
influential congregation, a congenial social life, and the possibility
that it would lead to an illustrious career.[18] But the suffering of the
East Enders, the sharp contrast between life in the East End and
West End of the city, was a moral challenge which he could not

ignore. Barnett was more willing to seek political solutions than
Geddes, openly supporting the radical and progressive elements of
the Liberal Party.[19] But ultimately he believed the challenge was
moral rather than political, the new wealth was undermining the
moral fibre of the city and nation, and only religion and social
service could counteract that.

'The passion for wealth', he was to write in *The Ideal City*, 'is
a new thing'[20] and he was not concerned with efforts to redistribute
wealth. Yet he wanted to overcome the moral turpitude of a society
which allowed the great contrasts of wealth and poverty to exist
side by side. He believed he could do this by suggesting that it was
the moral duty of the rich to provide a common social and cultural
environment in which all, rich and poor, could flourish within the
framework of a benevolent State. It was to be a crusade for the
benefit of the poor, to be carried out by the rich and privileged; in
Barnett's mind, a question of people before politics. These were the
views he put forward in the articles re-published in the volume
Practicable Socialism (1888).

Geddes and Barnett were nurturing their ideas on cities and city
development at a time when the demand for effective responses to
urban problems had never been higher. The mid-century years had
witnessed a great strengthening and widening of the powers of
central government, and the reform and development of local
government followed in its train. An attempt was made to improve
the social life and conditions of cities by providing a new framework
of legislation. Key elements in this were the Education Act of 1870
and the subsequent creation of an elementary system of education;
the Public Health Acts of 1872 and 1875, which made more public
health legislation compulsory and encouraged the growth of the
municipal civil service; and the reform of local government itself,
a concerted effort to provide democratic participation in local
government, and to iron out some of the anomalies of overlapping
jurisdiction of local authorities. Yet, in spite of all these fresh
departures, and whilst many improvements were made, conditions
in most cities deteriorated sharply in the poorer areas. The classic
indication of this was the figures given by Medical Officers of Health
for infant mortality in their cities, in which the contrast between
rich and poor areas was particularly striking. Legislation by itself

thus could not seem to make an impact on the economic and social evils of the slums.

In the sphere of philanthropy and voluntary social service, there had been a similar tendency towards greater efficiency, which met with similar discouragement. Voluntary workers found that problems outstripped their resources. The Charity Organisation Society of 1869, of which Canon Barnett was a founder member, had put all its effort into more efficient administration.[21] Yet the careful casework pioneered by its members revealed an inter-connection between poverty, bad environment and social problems which, for all their co-ordination of charitable effort and co-operation with Poor Law guardians, refused to be amenable to their solutions. Even the straightforward problem of relieving the high incidence of poverty amongst old people, first really established beyond a doubt by Booth's survey of the East End, was outside the frame of reference within which they worked. Their aim was to encourage the individual to be self-reliant and independent, and not to expect an old age pension as a right. Barnett, reluctantly, was forced to part company with C.O.S. on many issues.[22]

C.O.S. principles, however, found their way to many cities, including Edinburgh where an Edinburgh Social Union was founded in 1885. Geddes had helped to stimulate this development though not because he adhered to C.O.S. principles. Under the influence of his fiancee, Anna Morton, he had gone to London in 1884 to study philanthropic activity and particularly the ideas and work of Octavia Hill. The latter proved a far more decisive influence on him than the C.O.S.[23] Her attempt to rehabilitate old or deteriorated housing by better management, her enthusiastic support for the Kyrle Society, created by her sister Miranda to bring beauty and art to the poor, and her concern to preserve open spaces and historic environments (later organized as the National Trust for Preserving Places of Natural Beauty and of Historic Interest) were elements which strongly appealed to Geddes. He came back to Edinburgh to found an Environment Society to pursue similar aims to Miss Hill, but his more earnest philanthropic friends transformed this into the Edinburgh Social Union, organized on C.O.S. lines. Geddes then lost interest as he saw that the problems of Edinburgh, the problems of London and all large cities were not responding to treatment from the conventional sources of government and organized philanthropy. There was great demand for new ideas and a fresh approach.

This demand was intensified by a wider aspect of mass urbanization which was penetrating the thinking of many individuals in the second half of the century. This was the special cultural significance of a nation living mainly in cities and its implications for social progress in the future. The shift of the basis of a whole nation from being a mainly rural to a mainly urban dwelling people was enough to excite the imagination of those who saw social progress in terms of the future of modern civilization itself. The relationship between a national civilization and its component parts, the individual great cities, made such abstract concepts as civilization seem more tangible.[24] The essence of city life was that it was artificial and man-created, and as such it was not impossible to believe that it could be man-directed in the future. The power of this idea was to penetrate the social and political life of the nation at a myriad of points. Practical issues such as the clearance of slums, the provision of better housing, the relief of poverty, the improvement of education, thus become caught up in a wider debate on the nature of society and its direction in the future.

This has become a commonplace of twentieth-century politics. But in the late nineteenth century, this chance of self-direction on a practical basis still seemed intoxicatingly fresh, and not necessarily involved in politics. The failure of conventional methods for dealing with the social conditions of cities was a political issue, in which the extent and allocation of resources was of prime importance. But if the methods themselves were wrong, what should replace them was a challenge which politicians were singularly ill-prepared to meet. Fresh approaches could only be of two types: either a complete break with the past and the deliberate creation of a new urban environment; or a new insight into the forces shaping the cities as they are, as a prerequisite to controlling those forces. Both these possibilities were beyond politicians, involved in immediate short-term problems. The field was clear for the dreamers and philosophers, social scientists and social reformers to create their Ideal City, following one of the two approaches open to them, the ideal or reality, according to choice. Utopia or Eutopia were to be the blueprint for the future.

The appeal of Utopias is ever strongest at periods of rapid change and social tension, and many were created as a means of expressing a political and social criticism of the present.[25] The nineteenth century was particularly rich in their production with, perhaps, William Morris's *News from Nowhere* of 1890, and Ebenezer Howard's *Tomorrow: a peaceful path to social reform* of 1898 providing two outstanding examples of the genre at the time when the ideas of Geddes and Barnett were maturing. However, the Utopians of the late nineteenth century, who were seriously concerned with providing blueprints for the future, had to contend with a fundamental element, the concept of evolution, which their predecessors had been spared. As H. G. Wells wrote in his *Modern Utopia* (1905), the modern dreamer has to cope not only with the post-industrial revolution world, but also a post-Darwinian world: 'the Modern Utopia must be not static but kinetic, must shape not as a permanent state but as a hopeful stage, leading to a long ascent of stages. Nowadays we do not resist and overcome the great stream of things, but rather float upon it. We build now not citadels, but ships of state.'[26]

For those, like Barnett and Geddes, with a deep concern for social progress, civilization and the future, the appeal of an evolutionary Utopia was particularly strong. Utopia could be realized here and now, albeit at some lower stage of its fullest potential to bring happiness to all.[27] But if that lower stage was consciously and carefully chosen, that, in itself, provided some impetus towards achieving the next higher stage and thus uniting in one direction, social progress and the extension of civilization to the newly urban masses. It was a substitute for the framework of past, present and future which by now not only the classical economists but the sociologists as well had failed 'lamentably to produce. As practical reformers, both Barnett and Geddes used this evolutionary framework in terms of what was, what is, and what could be, always suggesting that the future grew from the present and was therefore a legitimate goal for present action. Further, they argued that this viewpoint put them outside the realms of modern politics. They believed that the great political debate between capitalist and socialist, whatever the outcome, was irrelevant to thinking creatively about urban living.

The arguments they used to support the last assumption were

remarkably similar. Both were conscious of the fact that in a modern industrial society, the problem of the future could ultimately be luxury, not want.[28] They were against the manufacture of wealth for the few and the exploitation of the masses; they were also against the redistribution of wealth, since all that would be achieved by this would be a debasement of the moral character of the working classes. What they wanted was a redistribution of wealth for the common good; a raising of civic life by common effort as this would elevate character and produce a higher civilization. Barnett suggested that 'the nationalization of luxury must be the object of social reformers'.[29] There was no want of means. The challenge was to find the way; as Barnett wrote, 'to discover the way is the problem of the times'.[30] The significance of the Ideal City to Barnett, or Eutopian Civics to Geddes, was that these were attempts to signpost the way.

Toynbee Hall and the Outlook Tower

The purpose of *The Ideal City* and 'Civics: as applied Sociology' then, was to make known practical ways of achieving social progress. These papers were the product of that interaction between thought and action that their authors had been advocating for years. Geddes made more attempt in his papers to provide a theoretical analysis of urban society than did Barnett, who was more interested in prescription than analysis in *The Ideal City*. Yet all these papers were the outcome of practical experience as much as any theory. Thus they need to be read in the light of Barnett's and Geddes's practical activities, particularly their involvement with their two institutions, Toynbee Hall and the Outlook Tower. These institutions were the apparatus which made the social experiments possible, and enabled both men to prescribe actions for the future with such confidence.

In *The Ideal City*, Barnett was careful not to mention his University settlement, claiming that he was concentrating only on the 'outward' elements of civic life, i.e. the ways of improving the physical environment.[31] Yet it was only knowledge of his achievements at Toynbee Hall which made the views he expressed in the pamphlet anything other than Utopian. Similarly, Geddes was listened to seriously by his audience at the first and second confer-

ences of the British Sociological Society, but only because he had
already acquired a reputation for his practical and educational work
in Edinburgh. Indeed, the context of their work and experience is
an essential element to an understanding of these papers. Thus,
instead of providing an analysis of their ideas alone, the rest of this
introduction will be devoted to tracing Barnett's and Geddes's
efforts to combine thought and action which, after all, was the
justification for taking their ideas seriously.

Since their vision of the Ideal City or Eutopia grew from, or was
inspired by, their activities at Toynbee Hall and the Outlook Tower,
their work at these institutions will provide the focus for analysis.
This does raise a problem since the two institutions were, on most
levels, strictly non-comparable. Toynbee Hall was a large-scale,
residential university settlement, with a religious purpose, which
became a forerunner of a movement spreading to many universities
and cities at home and abroad.[32] The Outlook Tower was merely a
small, civic museum, kept going by a few, mainly part-time enthu-
siasts, and no others were established on exactly the same pattern.
On one level, however, they can be compared. Both were described
as 'social laboratories'.[33] As Barnett and Geddes attempted a sociological approach to solving social problems, they were concerned
primarily with the city as a social environment. The main function
of Toynbee Hall and the Outlook Tower was to forward this work
and to provide ways of educating and instructing others on how to
extend their responses to city life.

'At this time of social transition', Geddes wrote, '. . . we all more
or less feel the melting away of old divisions and parties, of old
barriers of sects and schools, and the emergence of new possibilities,
the continual appearance of new groupings of thought and action.'[34]
What Barnett and Geddes were anxious about was whether the new
developments would lead to a higher civilization and social harmony,
or the reverse. Geddes's master, Le Play, had been one of the first
social scientists to undertake practical work in the cause of 'social
peace' and this objective was the aim of Barnett's and Geddes's work
and writing. The way they sought 'social peace' however, is strongly
contrasted in their papers. Geddes saw the problem as a natural
scientist.[35] His major concern was refuting what he considered were
over-hasty applications of Darwinist theory to the social sciences,

leading people to accept the prospect of conflict and struggle in the future as a natural part of the evolutionary process.

The key problem in evolutionary theory, even in the natural sciences, was to determine the prime movers, shaping the direction of change. Geddes's master, T. H. Huxley, had settled uncomfortably for the twin concepts of Nature red-in-tooth-and-claw, and the survival of the fittest, in his famous textbook of 1877 on evolution in the Thames basin.[36] Geddes, however, felt instinctively that Huxley was wrong since he approached the concept of evolution as a biological 'mechanical engineer' through the study of the bone structure of dead specimens.[37] Geddes wanted to study evolution in living organisms and for that he found the examples of co-operation and mutual aid in nature, collected by the natural scientist, geographer and Russian anarchist, Prince Peter Kropotkin, much more to his taste. In his activities at the Outlook Tower, he sought to establish co-operative enterprises and to encourage mutual aid as, potentially, the best way of achieving a higher social evolution.

As for Barnett, his conception of 'social peace' was much closer, if anything, to Le Play's. He believed passionately that the twin processes of industrialization and urbanization demanded from the capitalist and ruling classes ever greater degrees of effort to minimize any evil social consequences. He gained much support for Toynbee Hall in the first decade of its existence by lecturing and preaching tirelessly on the theme that the fate of the country would be decided in the next ten years and all depended on the upper classes doing their duty.[38] Their effort was to be directed not only to saving their own skins and maintaining the status quo, but in Barnett's eyes, to preserving the much more important objective, civilization as he understood it. Both Geddes and the Barnetts visited Paris in 1889 to attend the great international exhibition. One of the major exhibits, created by an old Le Playist disciple, M. Cheysson, Professor of Political Economy at the Ecole Libre des Sciences Politiques, was designed to illustrate the road to Social Peace, and it was dedicated to Le Play.[39] The need to work for 'social peace' was dramatically underlined for the Barnetts. They had to curtail their visit and return in haste to London, as their services were demanded to help solve the problem of the Great Dock Strike.

Barnett believed that his work at the Settlement could do what

'revolutions, missions and money have failed to do'.[40] He believed
that by living in the East End, he and his Residents could develop
a friendship based on trust with the poor and, on the other hand,
with their employers as well. The Warden of a Settlement would
have personal knowledge of local people and politics, a local reputation, acquaintance with other social workers especially the clergy
and 'what is more important of all, he would come into sympathy
with the hope, the unnamed hope, which is moving in the masses'.[41]
The path to reconciling conflicting interests and mounting aspira-
tions was the ideal of citizenship. This was his formula for 'social
peace'. It owed much to an idealized, Christian Socialist version of
England's rural past when squire, priest and villagers were purported
to have lived in harmony. Barnett wanted to create a socially mixed
local community in the East End in which community interests,
revealed through personal contact, would override the interests of
individuals and classes.

For Geddes, the road to 'social peace' was also built on an ideal
of citizenship. But his concept, whilst emphasizing the supreme
importance of the local community, was not based on the idea of
inter-class relationships. The three elements which Geddes brought
to his concept of citizenship rested on his position as an evolutionist,
natural scientist and last, but by no means least, a passionate
gardener. As an evolutionist, he sought for periods in history when
social harmony had appeared to prevail in cities and cultural life
had flourished. He then asked the evolutionist's question of 'how',
rather than the historian's 'why' this had happened. The result he
produced from this approach was as follows: the Industrial Revolution had caused the breakdown in the harmonious relationship
between man and his urban environment.[42] The initial impact of
industrialization, the growth of the factory system, an economy
based on steam power, coal and iron, he described as the Paleotechnic
era. The period of his own lifetime, with the development of gas and
electricity, more sophisticated machinery and materials, world wide
economic activity, better transport and communications, he labelled
the Neotechnic era. There was now more consideration for the
human individual, but Geddes wanted this to become the central
concern for the future in what he liked to call the incipient
'Eutechnic' era.

As a natural scientist, he believed the way towards the Eutechnic era lay in improving both the relationship between organism and environment and the quality of the organism itself. From Le Play, he had taken the basic elements of social life as Place, Work and Folk, and he tried to invent a way in which these three variables could be studied in the context of a city. Given the huge number of possible combinations of these variables, as numerous perhaps as the number of individuals living in the city, Geddes tried, on the one hand to create a simple theoretical framework for analysing quantities of data. He did this by inventing a 'thinking machine', a piece of paper folded into numbers of squares which could be filled in with the basic variables such as Place, Work and Folk and their relationships with each other. This notation was designed to help the user keep the widest possible perspective simultaneously on all subjects, and Geddes spent many hours developing it on to more complex levels.[43]

On the other hand, in the field of action, he emphasized the need for locally organized activities centred on a Tower or Civic Museum, where personal knowledge could create a sense of citizenship and personal contacts lead to co-operative activity.[44] Finally, what these activities should be, was suggested to him by his experience as a gardener, at least when he was concerned primarily with environmental improvement.[45] The key concept here was 'nurture', and Geddes put in hand schemes to develop waste land, to cultivate small open spaces, to clean, paint and decorate with sculpture houses, streets and neighbourhoods, and to remove eyesores and nuisances. This kind of work required voluntary support, in time and money, and this was what Geddes understood to be the ideal of 'citizenship'.

Barnett had modestly written that, with the kind of freedom a University Settlement offered, a born leader would 'discover means beyond our present vision'[46] for improving the condition of the poor. He did not put himself into this category and stuck prosaically to more conventional methods. But even if he lacked Geddes's imaginative abilities, his pursuit of conventional methods proved most creative. He mounted a three-pronged attack to improve the condition of the poor and to develop the potential for citizenship amongst his Residents, and it was this which he outlined again in

The Ideal City to guide Bristol's citizens. First, he had encouraged his Toynbee Residents to undertake public service in the capacity of local councillors, poor law guardians, school managers and other official but unpaid posts. He was able most forcibly to make the point that national legislation and the structure of local government in large cities depended for its application and day to day working on the services of a leisured class which in the poorer areas of large cities, such as the East End, simply did not exist. Toynbee Residents, under the stimulus of citizenship, could provide the missing leadership in public affairs.

Secondly, he encouraged Toynbee men to undertake philanthropic work. Under this category came the activities of the Charity Organisation Society, the support of local co-operative ventures, *ad hoc* committees such as the Sanitary Aid Committee of 1884, and societies dedicated to the discussion of social questions of which the Denison Club, founded in January 1885, was the earliest. Third and last, Barnett directed his own and his Residents' energies towards improving the recreational facilities of the East End for the poor. Under this last heading, Barnett fostered a number of activities with different objectives. He sent East End children to the countryside for summer holidays to bring them into contact with the purifying influences of Nature; he had a continual round of parties and social functions at Toynbee Hall as an effective method of helping East meet West and *vice versa*; and he attempted to create a number of cultural institutions, particularly the Whitechapel Public Library and Art Gallery to provide the East End with the same facilities necessary for a cultural life that were found in the West End. His vision of a higher civilization rested on the Arnoldian concept of Liberal Culture, all 'sweetness and light' and the pursuit of Beauty. A common culture shared by all was a prerequisite for the Ideal City.

As Barnett pursued these projects with a considerable degree of administrative ability and widespread support from Residents and philanthropists such as Passmore-Edwards,[47] he met with a good deal of success. Generations of Residents found themselves caught up in a hectic whirl of events, meetings and social functions which made Toynbee Hall appear to be the heart of the East End universe. For Barnett and his wife, it was the fulfilment of their dreams.

Barnett had struggled for ten years in the East End as Vicar of St Judes before he accepted the wardenship of Toynbee Hall in 1883. For ten years they had fought against the poverty, the slums, the sheer neglect that was to be found in their parish. Toynbee Hall brought them publicity and practical support. Under Barnett's gifted leadership, the influence of Toynbee Hall continued to grow, reaching a peak perhaps in the years from the early 1890s, when its success was assured, to Barnett's retirement in 1906. Barnett did not gain adequate recognition, in his wife's opinion, from the Church. But in 1893, he was made a Canon of Bristol Cathedral. It was this link which stimulated him to write *The Ideal City*, as an exercise in applying his recipe for the solution of the social problems of the East End to those of a great city.

Patrick Geddes, with his Outlook Tower, never achieved such influence and support. Yet roughly the same years, from about 1895 to 1910, marked the high peak of activities at the Outlook Tower, such as it was. Geddes has acquired the Tower in 1892, but it took two to three years to set it up as a Civic and Regional Museum and to work out its 'civic' function. This latter 'emerged' from a number of activities Geddes put in hand in his search for ways of encouraging social evolution in a direction which was progressive. His activities fell into three broad categories. The first were educational, especially the summer meetings held each year, which in the 1890s were devoted to the study of evolution in the natural and social sciences.[48] Secondly, he undertook a regional survey of Edinburgh as an exercise in applied social theory; and finally, he put his energies into developing the Outlook Tower. The Tower was to be a prototype of a Civic and Regional Museum which all cities should acquire since it was at once a repository of knowledge for the city, region and the world, and a culture power-house, generating by its activities a more 'scientific' interaction between citizen and the city, organism and environment, which would lead to a higher level of evolutionary development.[49]

The exhibitions at the Outlook Tower were designed to show in visual form how knowledge of one's city and region could provide a key to understanding the rest of the world.[50] The basis of such knowledge was firmly geographical. To emphasize this Geddes divided the rooms in the Outlook Tower in a descending order, from

Edinburgh and its region on the top floor, down through Scotland, English speaking countries, Europe, to the world on the ground floor. Geddes invented a general unit, the Valley Section, which encompassed a river from source to ocean outlet, covered the range of geographical features from mountain to river plain and the range of human settlements and occupations, from the shepherd in his croft to the complex commercial city at the mouth of the river.

Geddes was stimulated in his ideas by the work of the French regional geographers,[51] and at home by the Edinburgh tradition of map-making represented by the family firm of Bartholomews, experimenting in the 1890s with the new methods of illustrating the physical relief and resources of the world.[52] When another pioneer British geographer, H. J. Mackinder, was made director of the first British Institute of Geographical Studies at Oxford in 1899, Geddes tried, with Bartholomew's help, to get the Scottish Royal Geographical Society to support him and turn the Outlook Tower into a Scottish Geographical Institute.[53] Geddes's summer schools of 1904 and 1905 were devoted entirely to geography, but by then it was obvious that the money was not going to be forthcoming.

Partly this was no doubt due to the fact that Geddes's activities at the Outlook Tower were by no means limited to geography. In his Le Play formula for society, geography was only 'place', and 'work' entailed a study of economics, 'folk' a study of anthropology. To bring all these studies together in a specific context however, was a problem, and here Geddes, as an evolutionist and natural scientist, turned to the source of all knowledge for the school of 'vital' biologists to which he belonged, to the 'élan vital', the conception of Life as a unifying force. As he wrote: 'For with this fully biological outlook, geography and ecology, anthropology and evolution, are all at one in the understanding of Place, Work and People, in living interaction, psychological as well. And yet these are physical, biological and social, too. Life is the unity; its full study is synthetic; its analyses are but temporary divisions of labour, of which the results have ever to be incorporated into our under-standing of Life.'[54] Geddes's conception of Life as a unifying force was a close echo of Barnett's conception of Christianity and the power of God.[55] However, he had to work harder to justify it, and his attempt to utilize the whole repertoire of the natural and social sciences on his side, was not destined to allay the fears and suspicions of the Scottish Royal Geographical Society.

However, in the course of working out his ideas, Geddes developed the technique of the Regional Survey which was to be one of his major contributions to the town planning movement.[56] The problem both Geddes and Barnett faced was how to prescribe for a better future in the face of the problems of the present. The classic enunciation of those problems had been made by Charles Booth in his pioneering survey of the life and labour of London, which he carried out, incidentally, with the help of some Toynbee men amongst his other helpers.[57] Geddes however, sums up a common response to Booth's work, when he described the survey as a 'foggy labyrinth'.[58] He was full of admiration for Booth's attention to detail and accuracy, but the sum total of the work tended to bemuse rather than enlighten. There was no method there for informed social action. Both Barnett and Geddes gave considerable thought to this and their responses closely mirrored their different perspectives.

Starting from his concept of neighbourhood and personal contact between East and West, Barnett instituted a number of conferences at Toynbee Hall. Civil servants, politicians, social reformers and East Enders were brought together to discuss specific social problems such as poverty in old age, or low wages, in the context of the East End environment.[59] Geddes, starting from his concept of geographical region and social citizenship, conducted a number of Regional Surveys. The aim was to collect data of all aspects of life in the region, natural and social, economic and geographical, artistic and cultural. This information was then mounted as an exhibition and the sheer physical task of collecting data and hanging it, would produce a new understanding amongst the group of citizens engaged on this task. They would then develop specific views on such topics as the housing needs of the poor and recreational facilities. In other words, survey work would, by this special process, produce a plan for social action.[60]

Barnett's method was to work from the top downwards by trying to convince the ruling classes of the need for reform. Geddes's method was much more difficult to grasp. He was seeking a way in which reform and development could be generated from below, through the increased knowledge and participation of ordinary citizens. Barnett followed Booth by probing ever precisely into the range of problems relating to poverty and its relief, with special attention to low wages and unemployment.[61] The conferences and investigations on these and other topics held at Toynbee Hall, and the experience of Toynbee men in local government, gradually broke down Barnett's initial hostility to the state playing a greater role in solving social problems. To counter arguments that this was merely a new form of indiscriminate almsgiving which he, as a founder member of the C.O.S. in 1869, had fought so hard against, Barnett attached two conditions to his support for public action on poverty. The first was that the unit of administration should be the city and not the state. Civic social services would provide the context for the development of social citizenship amongst the ruling classes. The second was that such civic social services should be 'scientifically' administered. The ideal, as he clearly shows in *The Ideal City*, was a well-regulated city in which philanthropic zeal and public service would combine to create a healthy, stimulating environment in which the individual could flourish.[62]

Geddes on the other hand had a deep suspicion of regulations or any approach to city problems limited to specific areas. This, he thought, was a 'mechanical' response, and he wanted no more power to be given even to city authorities until they gave evidence that they understood the nature of the problems they had to deal with. For example, tackling specific problems in isolation could generate even worse problems for the future. His classic example of the result of such thinking was wholesale slum clearance programmes on the grounds of public health.[63] Geddes maintained with some force, that this was inefficient, even harmful in both the short and long term. It destroyed homes, leading to overcrowding elsewhere, it destroyed the economic and social balance of the neighbourhood, since large streets and expensive commercial sites replaced slum areas, and the problems of poverty and disease were merely pushed into a different area. In his plans for Indian cities, which were the only chance Geddes got for putting his ideas into practice, he emphasized that dirt was the cause of disease and that clean homes were the answer. The problem of the slum was both physical and social.[64] Physical obstacles to cleanliness – narrow airless courts, etc. – should be removed, but with as little damage to the ecological balance of the area as possible. On a social level, the housewife should be encouraged to be clean. In the longer term, open spaces should be provided, ideally some plots of land for individual cultivation, and the result would be a healthy city and healthy people on a permanent basis.

In spite of their totally divergent views on how to generate informal social action, the paths of Geddes and Barnett crossed more frequently in the early Edwardian period. Geddes, in 1903, gained his first commission to advise the Carnegie Dunfermline Trust on a plan for the layout of Pittencrief Park, gifted to the city with £500,000 by one of its erstwhile sons, Andrew Carnegie. Geddes became intoxicated with enthusiasm at this chance to put his ideas on civic development into practice and he far exceeded the limits of his commission. He canvassed over 200 leading social reformers, including Canon Barnett, with his ideas and his final report incorporated much more than just the park. He used its development as an excuse to project the social and physical evolution of the whole city. The Dunfermline burghers, however, proved hostile to ideas of social evolution; more hostile to Geddes's attempt to incorporate the whole town and all citizens in his schemes; and even more hostile to his idea of investing the bequest and only using the interest for small scale improvement schemes in perpetuity.[65] The rejection of his ideas pushed Geddes firmly back into the field of education and strengthened his intention to make London his base.

He was thus available to teach in a new School of Sociology, set up in London under the joint auspices of the Charity Organisation Society, the Settlement movement and the universities. The C.O.S. had been involved for many years in training their recruits and volunteers on a more professional basis.[66] Contacts with the Settlement movement and the universities grew as the demand for more information about social conditions spread. Barnett and other reformers were finding that the high peak of optimism they had enjoyed in the early 1890s was now beginning to fade. The publication of Rowntree's survey of York in 1901, and the findings of the committee on physical deterioration set up in 1904 to examine the evidence of unfitness of many of the volunteers for the Boer War, were just two of the more important indications that small progress had been made. Why were social problems still so acute 35 years after the founding of the Charity Organisation Society and 20 years after the Settlement movement had begun to develop? What social action could be taken? The optimism of the kind of prescriptions given in *The Ideal City* now seemed out of joint.

It was at this critical time that Geddes's friend and admirer, V. V. Branford, put up the money to found the British Sociological Society, which he hoped would be a vehicle for Geddes's ideas. Chamberlain's campaign for Tariff Reform, and attempts to link Imperialism with social reform, together with the determination of the Labour movement to do battle in face of the threat of the Taff Vale decision of 1901, put social issues back in the forefront of the political arena. Hopes were raised that the Sociological Society might produce some answers to social problems, and for the first two to three years of its existence, its meetings and conferences attracted a great deal of public attention.[67] Barnett and other Toynbee men such as E. J. Urwick and A. C. Haddon lent their authority and support to the new society. Geddes was invited to give papers in the first three sessions, and it was at the first two, in 1904 and 1905, that he presented his papers 'Civics: as applied Sociology'.

His aim was to provide a method of social action, angled not only towards solving social problems but also, more importantly in his view, pointing the way towards creating better norms of urban living. His technique was that of his Regional Survey, and his methodology, Le Play's Place, Work, Folk, incorporating all the social sciences.[68] At last, he had found the occasion and the influential audience to publicize his ideas. The disappointment was all the greater when he found he was met with a stunning, if polite, indifference. He was not alone in receiving this response. Other speakers could not fulfil the expectations that had been aroused and the early influential support for the British Sociological Society quickly faded as hoped-for panaceas for solving social problems failed to emerge.

Barnett was foremost amongst those seeking new solutions and he created a society at Toynbee Hall in 1904 – the Inquirers' Club.[69] This, unlike the Sociological Society, could concentrate on the social and political issues of the day without concerning itself with the problems of defining sociology as an academic subject. Research projects were put on foot and Barnett's expertise in collecting

politicians and experts together with his Residents and some East
Enders led to a number of well publicized conferences. Sometimes
the activities of the Inquirers' Club and the Sociological Society
overlapped, as on the occasion when Mrs Sidney Webb addressed
both groups on the subject 'Methods of Social Investigation'. W. H.
Beveridge, who succeeded Urwick as sub-warden at Toynbee in
1903, gave an early version of his views on the problems of the
unemployed to the Sociological Society in 1906.[70]

In many respects, however, 1904 had marked a watershed for
both Barnett and Geddes. Barnett had written a paper on 'Social
Reformers: past and present',[71] and he was full of lamentations for
what he sensed was a decline in the importance of the individual
social reformer. The element he singles out especially was the loss
of vision amongst men of goodwill. It was exactly this which had
been the dominant element in *The Ideal City*. He admits that in
many ways conditions had improved, though there was still plenty
to do. However, 'true' progress could only be achieved through
ideas; men needed to lift their eyes to the horizon as well as focusing
them on the immediate pressing problems. The cultural consensus
which had permitted the formulation of the vision of the *Ideal City*
in the early 1890s had been lost. Barnett saw around him, on the
one hand social conflict, on the other apathy to the public weal.
Even his great hope that more education would provide an answer
had begun to fade. By 1912 he wrote that the Universities' Experiment of Tutorial Classes for Working People was 'twenty years too
late. . . the race in all nations seems to be one between Education
and Ruin',[72] and he was far from sure that despite all his, and other
people's efforts, education was winning. As for the prospect of Ruin,
it meant the end of modern civilization as he understood it.

The vision of a higher civilization had, from the start, been the
foremost objective of his work. He had always understood that the
problems posed by urbanization were not simply those of dirt,
disease and poverty. Already these had been mainly confined to
specific areas, the slums, which was a residual problem, however
severe. The challenge was to create social harmony for the rest and
Barnett even welcomed the existence of the slums, in one respect,
in that they provided a context for social service and public effort.
He saw the function of social reform as the practical means for

widening the outlook of the country's rulers, whether they belonged
to the traditional governing classes or represented the newly enfran-
chised working-class majority. 'The danger of a democracy', he
wrote, 'is lest deprived of that impulse, that habitual watchfulness
which accompanies the strife between the Few and the Many, it
may settle down in a somewhat sordid comfort of arm-chairs and
abundant food, and cease to make progress.'[73] Progress towards a
higher civilization needed total commitment, vision and personal
sacrifice.

Geddes shared Barnett's view on the race between Education and
Ruin. But his vision of progress towards a higher civilization was
largely unsullied by any consideration of politics. Yet his allegiance
to the social sciences and especially to geography had alerted him
to the greatest danger potentially to his dreams of achieving Eutopia.
In 1904 H. J. Mackinder published his famous article in the
Geographical Journal, 'The Geographical Pivot of History', in
which he suggested that for the first time the world's statesmen
needed to take into account the 'real proportion of features and
events on the stage of the whole world' as the world was now an
integrated economic unit. His message was that the competition for
the world's resources amongst industrialized countries contained a
political element, and he saw future conflict in 'the great economical
struggle between the great inside core of the Euro-Asiatic continent
and the smaller marginal regions and islands outside'.[74] He was
adding a geographical element to the arms race which made world
war seem an inevitability.

Geddes had already developed a preoccupation with war, particularly since the Paris International Exposition of 1900. An exhibit
there on the prospect of war produced by a leading pacifist, M. Jean
Bloch, had particularly fascinated him. He had got a group of
volunteers from the Outlook Tower to move the exhibit to a
permanent home in Lausanne as he thought it was so outstandingly
important.[75] He maintained a war exhibit at the Outlook Tower and
introduced amongst his other activities a Current Affairs Club. Here
the economic and social issues of the world, as reported in the press
and up-to-date publications, were collected and the data displayed
in an exhibition. Geddes understood the power of nationalism allied
to self-interest, and he tried to warn others of the potential danger.[76]

Whilst he was totally hostile to war, however, he was fascinated by the social effects of war. The welding together of a nation at times of war and the co-operative spirit created by a common objective which united the unnamed masses, was exactly the kind of spirit Geddes wanted to generate and harness for his civic renewal.[77] When the First World War did break out, Geddes held a number of conferences and instituted a series of monographs on the subject of the making of the future, trying to capitalize on the war spirit, though without much success.[78] This could have been because, although Geddes loved the comradeship of wartime, his message was anti-nationalistic, anti-government, anti-regimentation of any kind, which in essence, was the exact opposite of what actually happened to the economy and society during the war. Yet Geddes was able to keep his vision and his hope for progress because his starting point for change was the potential for a better world inherent in a modern technological society.

In such a society, he believed that the need for centralized government would soon appear obsolete. The road to progress and a higher civilization was to be found in co-operation amongst individuals on some local initiative. He wanted cities, towns, villages, groups and associations to work out their own regional salvation. They needed freedom to develop their own ideas and the vision to plan. Diagnosis must precede prescription and both should be carried out by those with an intimate knowledge of the problems and area. The means could be found locally, an aspect of his vision which would have met with Barnett's warm approval, though Geddes did not think in terms of any costly capital expenditure. His general aim was to unite individuals in common civic action, making them more socialized, and on the other hand, to encourage communities to develop separately, thus making them more individualized.[79] This was the vision behind his two papers on 'Civics: as applied Sociology', and he had the great good fortune to find, in spite of his lack of success with the Sociological Society, some ardent support for his programme of social action from a small band of young men for whom idealism and vision were of the first importance.

These young men were caught up with, and anxious to promote, the cause of town planning in Britain. Geddes was able to form a

Civics Committee of the Sociological Society with their support, and
he launched himself with zest into this movement which seemed to
share his optimism for the future if not his particular conception
of civics. The movement towards town planning, created from the
converging interests of specific groups such as the housing reformers,
municipal authorities and sanitarians,[80] was nevertheless nurtured
in the soil of that middle-class idealism, that spirit of goodwill,
which Barnett had so effectively harnessed for Toynbee Hall. Here
there was no social conflict, since town planning was largely outside
the main arena of political debates. There was no legislation cutting
across individual property rights or burdening the rates, and the
ideal of environmental improvement could be shared by all social
classes. Geddes had followed his Civics papers at the third session
of the Sociological Society in 1906 with a paper trying to arouse
support for a Civic Museum or Exhibition in London.[81] Once again
he failed, but his energies found an outlet in training his small Civics
Committee in the techniques of his Regional Survey. They, in their
turn, were to form the backbone of the loosely federated Regional
Survey Association when it was formed in 1914.[82]   The idea of
survey work was already fashionable in the Edwardian period, made
so by the work of Booth and Rowntree. Mrs Barnett wrote with
some acerbity that 'it was more easy to obtain the volunteer services
of men and women eager to investigate conditions than to reform
them, or rescue their consequent human wreckage'.[83] Geddes's survey
technique however, was different. The geographical approach to the
city and its regions was a method of understanding the city in its
totality. The sociological data collected was designed to be the
preliminary to informed social action. Geddes's Place, Work, Folk,
seemed to be providing the way towards making the modern city
intelligible to the individual. This was the attraction for town
planners of his Regional Survey.[84] The other prophets of the town
planning movement such as Ebenezer Howard, and even its practical
practitioner Raymond Unwin (at work in these years building Mrs
Barnett's Hampstead Garden Suburb), operated to some extent
outside the 'normal' conditions of the large industrial city. The
general woolliness of Geddes's concepts, the level of generality at
which he worked, could be forgiven because of this special contribution. He stood alone in his attempt to relate the physical envi-

ronment to the social structure of the community. He was the only founder member of the Town Planning Institute described as a sociologist.

Yet Geddes's 'sociology' bore little resemblance to the academic discipline of that name. Geddes, like Barnett, had a profound interest in social factors, but only in so far as they could be shaped by positive social action to lead to a better future. The high point of Geddes's career came when, at last, he got his civics exhibition and was appointed as the Director of the Cities and Town Planning Exhibition in 1910. This exhibition, originally mounted to publicize the 1909 Act amongst British municipalities, he made his own, filling it with material from the Outlook Tower and prolonging its life after the initial exhibition period was over. He made it into a travelling exhibition to take to large cities anywhere, at their invitation, offering explanatory notes and a series of lectures to elucidate the meaning from the mass of material he displayed. The ideas and technique were those he describes in his Civics paper which he had developed at his Outlook Tower and at his special international summer school at the Paris Exposition of 1900.[85] He gained his greatest international accolade in 1913, winning the Gold Medal at the International Exposition at Ghent, which was devoted to a concern for social conditions and urban development.

The town planners, municipal administrators, civil servants, professional and business people from Europe and America who visited the exhibition were spellbound by Geddes's range of material, broad interpretations and confident predictions for the future.[86] His own view of his Cities and Town Planning Exhibition was the same as for his Outlook Tower with its attendant activities of Regional Survey. He saw it as a social laboratory buttressed by 'scientific' experiment, parallel in nature and purpose to the scientific laboratories and practical experiments which had produced the revolution in the study of the sciences and natural sciences in the nineteenth century. The dynamic factor behind all his work, however, was his belief in evolution, both in the natural and social sciences. He saw his special 'sociological conception of the city as, in a very real sense, a natural, i.e. an evolutionary growth, which makes each civic Eutopia a rational forecast, and its realisation, however partial in our time, a worthy and an immediate aim'.[87]

To create a 'scientific' social laboratory had been one of Barnett's fundamental aims in setting up Toynbee Hall. His ambitions had been similar to those of Geddes, even if he had put his hopes for future enlightenment on the spirit of goodwill of his Residents, rather than the development of a synthesis of the natural and social sciences. In his view, the vision of the future would be produced in the minds of Residents, through a combination of detailed knowledge, personal experience and a sympathetic imagination. In the early exhilarating days of the settlement movement, in 1889, a paragraph of the Toynbee Annual Report had read: 'The object of Toynbee can never be fully realised if the attempt is not made to render the Hall more and more a repository of systemized facts, relating to the complex life and varied social and economic problems that East London presents. And if the results of special investigations and gleanings from the varied knowledge that is floating in the minds of many at the Hall, can be made generally accessible, Toynbee will have provided, not only valuable information of an academic kind, but more of the *truth* upon the knowledge of which wise action must be based.'[88]

Barnett and Geddes had both tried to face the complexities of modern city life, not in order to define or analyse it, but in order to promote informed social action. Such action was directed not only towards solving social problems, but even more towards creating a higher civilization for all. Both were convinced that action on immediate problems, without well formulated, longer term objectives, created fresh and greater difficulties for the future. Both wanted to develop a wider outlook on the city, and to encourage a vision of the potential of modern city life to provide the best, not the worst environment for man. Barnett's 'Ideal City', and Geddes's 'Eutopia' with their personal idiosyncrasies and, perhaps, false optimism, share one vital element. They were not merely abstract ideas. They were based on the practical experience of men who had devoted their lives to improving the physical, social and cultural environment of cities. The significance of the following texts lies precisely in this fact. Their emphasis on an interaction between theory and practice in their approach towards an understanding of city life was the most important element Barnett and Geddes bequeathed to those working after them in the fields of social administration and town planning. The fact that Britain in the twentieth century took a different path in these fields from other countries owed not a little to their work.

NOTES

1. Barnett was nicknamed 'The Prophet' by his inner circle of Residents and T. Edmund Harvey wrote that the name was no idle one. H. O. Barnett, *Canon Barnett, his life, work and friends* (1921 Cheaper edition), (all page references will be to this edition), 317. The first book on Geddes, published in his lifetime, was A. Defries, *The Interpreter Geddes: the Man and his Gospel* (1927).

2. H. O. Barnett, *op. cit.*, 772–82. Personal tribute was paid to Geddes at the Sir Patrick Geddes Centenary Celebrations, Oct. 1954 (pamphlet, Edinburgh College of Art) by Sir Patrick Abercrombie, Sir William Holford and Professor H. J. Fleure amongst others.

3. W. G. Briody, 'A Preliminary Inquiry into the ideas of Patrick Geddes', *Papers in Urban and Regional Studies*, I (C.U.R.S., Birmingham, 1977) criticizes Geddes for failing to take into account strong social and political forces.

4. S. A. Barnett, 'Our present discontents', *The Nineteenth Century and After*, Feb. 1913, reprinted in *Practicable Socialism*, new series (1915). Geddes, in his last book, recounts a dream in which he is failing to communicate his ideas to a living soul. P. Geddes and J. A. Thomson, *Life: Outlines of Biology* (1931), 1417–18.

5. For a discussion on the concept of community see R.A. Nisbet, *The Sociological Tradition* (1967), 47.

6. Descriptions of Geddes's activities are to be found in three biographies. P. Boardman, *Patrick Geddes: Maker of the Future* (Chapel Hill, 1944) and *The Worlds of Patrick Geddes* (1978); P. Mairet, *Pioneer of Sociology: the Life and Letters of Patrick Geddes* (1957); and P. Kitchen, *A Most Unsettling Person: An Introduction to the Ideas and Life of Sir Patrick Geddes* (1975).

7. Arnold Toynbee's famous words provided Barnett with his credo: 'Any attempt to preach a purer religion must go along with attempts at social reform... progress will never be organic until the religious spirit breathes through every act and institution.' A. Milner, *Arnold Toynbee: A Reminiscence*, 27, quoted from K. S. Inglis, *Churches and the Working Classes in Victorian England* (1963), 150.

8. See Walter L. Creese, *The Search for Environment: The Garden City, Before and After* (New Haven, 1966).

9. For responses to poverty in London in the 1880s see G. S. Jones, *Outcast London: a study in the relationship between classes in Victorian Society* (1971), 285.

10. A collection of his essays under the title *Methods of Social Reform* was published in 1883 shortly after his untimely death.

11. J. M. Keynes, *Essays in Biography* (1951), 137 and 151–3.

12. H. S. Foxwell, 'The Economic Movement in England', *Quarterly Journal of Economics*, 1887.

13. C. Bibby, *T. H. Huxley: Scientist, Humanist and Educator* (1959).

14. 'A true theory of social progress is not a cause of movement but simply oil to the movement – serves simply to remove friction. The force producing the movement is the aggregate of men's instincts and sentiments, and these are not to be changed by a theory.' Quoted from J. D. Y. Peel, *Herbert Spencer: the evolution of a sociologist* (1971), 164.

15. G. S. Jones, *op. cit.*, 159–78.

16. Geddes subscribed to a brand of 'technological romanticism' prevalent in the late nineteenth century, which held that technology would solve all problems. He believed, in the company of others such as William Morris, that electric power and small machines, individually operated, would lead to the decentralization of economic units in a way directly opposite to the impact of steam power.

17. 'The Classification of Statistics and its results', *Proceedings of the Royal Society of Edinburgh*, 1881; 'Economics and Statistics considered from the point of view of the preliminary sciences', *Nature*, Sept. 1881; 'Analysis of the Principles of Economics', *Proceedings of the Royal Society of Edinburgh*, 1884; *John Ruskin, Economist* (pamphlet, Edinburgh, 1884); *Conditions of progress of the capitalist and the labourer* (pamphlet, Edinburgh, 1886); *Cooperation versus Socialism* (pamphlet, Manchester, 1888).

18. In 1872 he was offered a living near Oxford. H. O. Barnett, *op. cit.*, 66.

19. A trip to America in 1867, where Barnett found city life totally neglected and all energies devoted to private gain, formed his political opinions. He wrote: 'Born and nurtured in an atmosphere of Toryism, what I saw and heard there knocked all the Toryism out of me.' *ibid.*, 13.

20. See below, *The Ideal City*, |12|.

21. C. L. Mowat, *The Charity Organisation Society 1869–1913: its ideas and work* (1961).

22. In 'Practicable Socialism' (1883), Barnett advocates old age pensions. His final split with the C.O.S. came in 1895, after a public confrontation with C. S. Loch, Secretary of the C.O.S. H. O. Barnett, *op. cit.*, 655–60.

23. This was an influence which Barnett more than shared. Barnett had met Miss Hill in 1868 and worked very closely with her during the

next five years. They remained life-long friends, and shared a similar
approach to social problems.

24. For a discussion of some of the social implications of this see H. E.
Meller, *Leisure and the Changing City* (1976), 6–16.
25. See W. H. G. Armytage, *Heavens Below: Utopian Experiments in
England 1560–1960* (1961).
26. H. G. Wells, *A Modern Utopia* (1905), 5.
27. Barnett states in *The Ideal City*, 5, 'My object is to put before you
a pattern, an Ideal City, *which is not beyond your reach.*'
28. An idea central to John Ruskin's economic and social writings. See
J. C. Sherburne, *John Ruskin, or the Ambiguities of Abundance: A
study in Social and Economic Criticism* (Cambridge, Mass., 1972).
29. 'Town Councils and Social Reform', in *Practicable Socialism* (1888),
65.
30. *Ibid.*, 67.
31. See below, *The Ideal City*, |14|.
32. See J. A. R. Pimlott, *Toynbee Hall: Fifty Years of Social Progress
1884–1934* (1935).
33. H. O. Barnett, *op. cit.*, 323. Charles Zueblin (Chicago University)
described the Outlook Tower as 'The World's First Sociological Laboratory', *American Journal of Sociology*, iv, no. 5, 1889, 577–92.
34. See below, 'Civics', Pt. II, |111|.
35. Although after the 1880s, Geddes worked and published mainly in the
social sciences, he remained Professor of Botany at the University
College of Dundee, St Andrews, from 1889 to 1919. The chair, especially
endowed for him by J. Martin White, was only part-time however,
under the terms of his contract, leaving him free for nine months
each year.
36. T. H. Huxley, *Physiography* (1877).
37. P. Geddes and V. Branford, *The Coming Polity* (Maker of the Future
series), (1917), 1–11.
38. H. O. Barnett, *op. cit.*, 415.
39. T. N. Clark, *Prophets and Patrons: The French University and the
Emergence of the Social Sciences* (Cambridge, Mass., 1973),
108–11.
40. S. A. Barnett, 'University Settlements', *op. cit.*, 99.
41. *Ibid.*, 103.
42. P. Geddes, *Cities in Evolution: an introduction to the Town Planning Movement and the Study of Civics* (1915), 60–83.
43. See below, 'Civics', Pt. II, |72|.
44. *Ibid.*, |109–11|.
45. His fullest discussion of this is to be found in his Dunfermline Report,
City Development, a study of parks, gardens and culture-institutes
(1904) Section B, Chapters IV–X. He suggests that 'city improvers,
like the gardeners from whom they develop, fall into two broadly

contrasted schools, which are really, just as in gardening itself, the formal and the naturalistic.' Both can be followed with advantage.

46. S. A. Barnett, 'University Settlements', *op. cit.*, 104.

47. Who, amongst other benefactors, provided £5,000 for the building of the Whitechapel Art Gallery. H. O. Barnett, *op. cit.*, 566.

48. See P. Boardman, *Esquisse de l'oeuvre educatrice de Patrick Geddes* (Montpellier, 1936), esp. 53–61.

49. Geddes translated the evolutionary formula of environment, function, organism (efo) into a social doctrine which he described as 'the joint regionalist-humanist doctrine', i.e. efo in human society. Two volumes in the Making of the Future series were dedicated to publicizing this 'doctrine': V. Branford, *Interpretations and Forecasts: a Study of Survivals and Tendencies in Contemporary Society* (1914) and P. Geddes and V. Branford *The Coming Polity.* See pp. 56–7 in the latter.

50. Geddes had two basic aims in his educational activities: to reach everyone regardless of age, intelligence or education; secondly, to encourage participation in environmental projects. He used visual materials and models to achieve the former, and his exhibitions were neither orderly nor complete to encourage the latter. Another exponent of these techniques for similar purposes was T. C. Horsfall, President of the Manchester Citizens Association. Barnett admired Horsfall's visual approach very much. H. O. Barnett, *op. cit.*, 555.

51. See L. Febvre, *A Geographical Introduction to History* (1925), 19.

52. C. B. Muriel Lock, *Geography: a reference handbook* (1972 ed.), 59–60.

53. J. G. Bartholomew, 'Plea for a National Institute of Geography', P. Geddes, 'Note on Draft Plan for Institute of Geography' and 'Nature Study and Geographical Education', *Scottish Geographical Magazine*, XVIII, 1902.

54. P. Geddes and J. A. Thomson, *Life: Outlines of Biology* (1931), 2 vols., 1403.

55. Barnett, as a curate, had held the opinion that 'religious teaching was too much a religion of death' and that what was wanted was a 'religion of life'; and his wife wrote that 'he held that the Church should be the centre of life, that all men should be counted as belonging to it, and that "its teaching should permeate every department of action".' Barnett wrote to his fiancee in 1872, 'Life in nature and life in humanity must be our stimulus.' H. O. Barnett, *op. cit.*, 24–5 and 65.

56. 'Edinburgh and its region, Geographic and Historical', *Scottish Geographical Magazine*, XVIII, 1902.

57. See P. Abrams, 'The Tradition of Booth' in *The Origins of British Sociology 1834–1914* (Chicago, 1968), 136–43.

58. See below, 'Civics', Pt. II, |104|.

59. H. O. Barnett, *op. cit.*, 451.

60. P. Geddes, 'Beginnings of a survey of Edinburgh', *Scottish Geograph-ical Magazine*, Vol. 35, 1919, esp. 297.

61. He was chairman of the 1907 West Ham survey which was directed towards revealing the evils of the casual labour system. This survey has been described by Abrams as representing as closely as any single study could 'British sociology in its first period'. Abrams, *op. cit.*, 151.

62. Canon and Mrs S. A. Barnett, *Towards Social Reform* (1909), esp. 11–12.

63. P. Geddes, *Cities in Evolution* (1915), 150.

64. J. Tyrwhitt (ed.), *Patrick Geddes in India* (1947), 45.

65. Geddes papers, ms 10612 and 10536, National Library of Scotland, Edinburgh.

66. H. Bosanquet, *Social Work in London 1869–1912* (1914), 400–5.

67. R. J. Halliday, 'The Sociological Movement, the Sociological Society and the Genesis of Academic Sociology in Britain', *Sociological Review*, XVI, 1968.

68. A survey of his thinking leading up to the writing of these papers is to be found in H. E. Meller, 'Patrick Geddes: an analysis of his theory of civics, 1880–1904', *Victorian Studies*, XVI, 1973.

69. J. A. R. Pimlott, *op. cit.*, 104, and H. O. Barnett, *op. cit.*, 447.

70. *Sociological Papers*, Vol. III, 1906, 323–32.

71. Reprinted in *Towards Social Reform*, 19–25.

72. 'A Race between Education and Ruin', in *Practicable Socialism*, new series (1915), 333–4.

73. 'Introduction', *Towards Social Reform* (1909), 17–18.

74. He developed these ideas into a monograph after the First World War, *Democratic ideals and reality: a study in the politics of reconstruction* (1919). They were to influence deeply Hitler's army generals in the 1930s.

75. Geddes and Slater, *Ideas at War* (1917), 31.

76. See Chapter III, 'World-Cities and their opening competition' in *Cities in Evolution* (1915), 46–59.

77. 'People volunteer for war; and it is a strange and dark superstition that they will not volunteer for peace', *ibid.*, 101.

78. Geddes took part in the morale-boosting Reconstructed City Exhi-bition in Paris 1916.

79. A 'popular' version of his 'regionalist-humanist' doctrine is to be found in a series of pamphlets, published 1917–19, as suitable infor-mation for propaganda lectures on civics, with slides available on request. Entitled 'Papers for the Present', they were produced by the Civics Committee of the Sociological Society. No. 9 in the third series, *The Drift to Revolution*, contains all the ideas outlined here.

80. W. Ashworth, *The Genesis of Modern British Town Planning* (1954), 167–90.

81. Published in *Sociological Papers*, Vol. III, 1906, 197–237.

82. I. C. Davies, J. Fraser and W. Mann, 'The Regional Association and its Mode of Work', *Sociological Review*, Spring 1920. Geddes's regionalism was related to his world outlook. After the First World War, he wanted to encourage connections between cities and their regions across the barriers of nation states. He wrote to his friend Henri Bergson, then President of the League of Nations Committee for Intellectual Co-operation, to float the idea of a world federation of cities.

83. H. O. Barnett, *op. cit.*, 445.

84. Through his Regional Survey approach, Geddes took for granted that town planning was concerned with the whole range of life and activity in a town. W. Ashworth, *op. cit.*, 198.

85. P. Boardman, *op. cit.*, 95–102.

86. A vivid description of Geddes's exhibit at Ghent is given by A. Defries, who was there, in her monograph *The Interpreter Geddes: the man and his gospel* (1927), 57–78.

87. 'A Suggested Plan for a Civic Museum (or Civic Exhibition) and its associated studies', *Sociological Papers*, Vol. III, 1906, 229.

88. H. O. Barnett, *op. cit.*, 446 (my italics).

NOTE TO *THE IDEAL CITY*

His wife described Canon Barnett's *Ideal City* as a 'charming pamphlet' and said that he wrote it hoping 'to awaken the pride which is both "humble and inspired"'. It was obviously written in a spirit of much affection for his native city. Yet Barnett was also very much in earnest. When he was appointed a Canon of Bristol Cathedral, this was the first major recognition of his work made by the Church he served, and he and Mrs Barnett considered carefully whether or not they should leave Whitechapel after 20 years of service there and take up residence permanently in Bristol. In the end, they decided against it, and throughout the period of his Bristol canonry, from 1893 to 1906, Barnett remained an 'absentee' Canon, visiting the city for only three months every year. However, the decision to return to Whitechapel was made only after careful consideration of which location would benefit most from Barnett's services. To make an informed decision, Barnett had devoted his first few stays in Bristol to studying the educational, industrial and philanthropic conditions of the city. His knowledge of the city, when he came to write *The Ideal City*, was thus based on personal research.

The Ideal City was meant to outline a course of practical action, rather than to be a manifesto of Barnett's social philosophy. All the ideas it contains had been the staples of Barnett's message to the world, at least since the 1880s, when the founding and development of Toynbee Hall had provided him with a public platform. His object in writing it was to put before the citizens of Bristol 'a pattern, an Ideal City, which was not beyond (their) reach'. His pattern or formula, was based on two assumptions; that ideas were more important than resources in the regulation and improvement of city life; and that what was best in such a life could be defined in terms of the ideal of Liberal Culture. His social vision was completely dominated by his own middle class origins and his appeal, in *The Ideal City*, was to those in positions of power and influence in Bristol who would naturally share his viewpoint. His little pamphlet was a propaganda piece on what could be done by the ruling classes of the city if they had the vision and will-power to direct their energies towards civic improvement.

The Ideal City was in the genre, albeit a Church of England example, of the literature and sermons of the Nonconformist 'civic gospel' created in Birmingham in the 1860s. However, writing 30 years later, Barnett was able to draw upon the growing body of knowledge of urban social problems and ways of combating them. Yet he shared with the 'civic gospel' of Dawson, Crosskey and Dale, two fundamental beliefs: that the hope for progress in the life of any city depended in the last resort on 'the religious sense of its individuals', and secondly, that the cultural life of a nation was nurtured in cities. Civilization, or the development of Art from Life, was an urban product. The Birmingham 'civic gospellers' had excited their audiences by dwelling not on the new Jerusalem, but on 'the glories of Florence and the other cities of Italy in the Middle Ages' which contemporary Birmingham might try to emulate. Barnett, emphasizing the cultural ideals, also suggests that the 'highest possible life for men may be a city life'.

Two-thirds of the pamphlet is devoted to making a case for these beliefs to stimulate the essential motivation for action. The arguments provide a summary of the ideas contained in the volume entitled *Practicable Socialism: essays on Social Reform* which Barnett had published with his wife in 1888. In *The Ideal City* however, Barnett goes beyond the limitations of his *Practicable Socialism* essays, which are each devoted to specific subjects, and attempts a total approach. Focus is given to his ideas by Barnett's use of Bristol, and he emphasizes the practical nature of his vision by providing his Ideal City with those physical attributes already enjoyed by Bristol.

The main arguments Barnett uses for motivating action can be summarized as follows: first, there is a stress on the importance of the quality of the environment. 'Life is more than its environment, but its environment does influence life'. Thus environmental factors are a proper concern for social reformers. Secondly, the problem of poverty, so evident in inner city areas, is a problem of neglect. If an adequate support system of voluntary and municipal social institutions were available, no individual would fall into poverty as, better educated, and strengthened by wholesome recreation, all would have a chance to earn a living for themselves. Lack of such institutions signified neglect and a lack of social concern amongst the rich and the educated. Neglect could only be overcome by personal care, and the right kind of knowledge which was moral as well as factual, and such knowledge could only be transmitted by personal commitment.

This is one of the most important themes in *Practicable Socialism*, especially in Barnett's essay on 'University Settlements'. In *The Ideal City*, however, Barnett deliberately underplays this argument, stating 'here I am trying to trace possible changes in outward things, and their effect on the happiness and character of people'. In the *Ideal City* the emphasis is on attainable improvements to the physical environment, even though Barnett himself believed that the main virtue in carrying out all the ideas he puts forward was to create the means for the rich to serve the poor. This was the purpose of social reform and this was the only hope for peaceful social development in the future. However, Barnett 'externalizes' his argument, by putting forward the ideal of a great civilization. In his ideal society, wealth is used not for private ostentation but for public welfare; and rich and poor share a common life in which people will have pleasure in their work, and leisure to admire what is beautiful.

Barnett, perhaps more than any other social reformer, appreciated the fact that city life gives form to the economic and social inequalities of society. His work in London's East End had taught him to see the vicious circle of deprivation which kept the poorest areas of the city with the greatest social problems, the least well equipped to deal with them, both in resources and manpower. His experience had also given him an insight into that great divide in the nineteenth-century system for the relief of poverty between the 'deserving' and the 'undeserving'. Even whilst he was confirming his belief that the main causes of poverty amongst the 'undeserving' were moral failings of character, he was honest enough to see that the reward for being 'deserving' in modern society was very little. The life of the 'deserving' poor, the endless struggle against hopeless odds for no rewards this side of heaven, engaged his full sympathy. His dedication to providing educational and recreational institutions for the poor of similar quality to those enjoyed by the rich, stemmed from his strong sense of the need for social justice. A great civilization could only develop from a just society in which 'Art will grow out of common life' emanating from the masses and enjoyed by all.

Barnett's vision of a great civilization, however, was as far removed from illustrious and often-quoted precursors such as Florence in the Middle Ages, as his vision of the role of Toynbee Hall was from his idealized view of the role of parson and squire in a rural parish. Barnett's great civilization was a modern one in which the administration of cities was efficient and extended over all areas affecting the social life of citizens. It was one in which modern technology was to be made socially less harmful and even harnessed towards providing new social benefits; it was one in which wealth, being so abundantly produced, was to be used to enrich the lives of all and not just the few, the owners of capital. The point Barnett makes with considerable force several times in *The Ideal City*, is that such developments did not require any fundamental changes in human beings themselves, or in the political organization of society. He believed that goodwill was a feature of human nature to be found at all levels of society, and that social revolution would not bring the masses one jot nearer to those practical improvements which could transform the quality of urban living. What is more, such improvements were already within reach.

The last third of his pamphlet Barnett devotes to outlining those practical projects which could all be achieved with a liberal interpretation of existing permissive legislation. He addresses himself to the Town Council, the School Board and the Poor Law Board of Guardians. In his paper in *Practicable Socialism* on 'Town Councils and Social Reform', Barnett states his belief that these locally elected bodies represented Society, and that if these bodies engaged in civic improvements, this was more socially healthy than individuals and societies doing the same work, who might be accused of vested interests. The best method for attaining social reform was a framework of national legislation, carried out and adapted by locally elected bodies. It was least likely to affect the spirit of energy and independence of the rich, and to pauperise the poor by offering largesse indiscriminately. Barnett thus established his own position in the contemporary debate on whether voluntary agencies or the state were · the most appropriate agents for pioneering social improvements. He placed his faith in the energy and initiative of locally elected bodies.

The list he provides in *The Ideal City* of suitable objectives for local bodies, however, was certainly eclectic. The first concern of the Town Council should be with housing. This does not only reflect Barnett's belief in the family as the corner-stone of society. His brother, Francis Gilmour Barnett, was active in local politics in Bristol as a progressive Liberal town councillor in the 1880s and 1890s, and was particularly concerned with housing. Bristol had not adopted the Torrens and Cross Acts of 1867 and 1875, and only gradually adopted bye-law regulations in a piecemeal fashion in the 1890s under pressure from the Bristol Committee for Promoting the Better Housing of the Poor, formed in 1890. After housing, Barnett listed the removal of nuisances and the creation of positive cultural influences, such as noble and inspiring buildings as prerequisites for the good life. He was also ready to tilt at religious pedants with his demand for the Sunday opening of libraries and museums. His concern was directly with the physical and social well-being of all citizens, the latter being determined by standards of 'respectable' behaviour and a taste for recreation cultivated according to the precepts of Liberal Culture.

His recommendations for the School Board and the Poor Law Guardians were confined to his own special concerns. Elementary education should be made more attractive to children so that they would pursue cultural activities in their adult life, and it should have a practical bias since the majority were going to be manual workers. Brighter children should have an opportunity to stay at school until 14 or 15 years of age. As for the Poor Law, Barnett confined himself mainly to his particular hobby horse, which was old age pensions. He had advocated old age pensions as a better alternative to indoor or outdoor relief several years before Charles Booth established old age as a major cause of poverty in the East End. A Royal Commission was appointed in 1895 to study the problems of the Aged Poor, but it did not recommend universal old age pensions. Since unemployment and sickness were also causes of poverty, Barnett wanted Poor Law authorities to take more appropriate action by combatting the causes, as well as relieving the poverty, they entailed. Finally, the greatest social evil, Drink, should be the concern of the local magistrates who could act by closing down the excessive number of drink shops in the city.

Barnett was ready to admit that his civic improvements would cost money. What he tries to prove in *The Ideal City* is that public and private resources were available if they were properly used. Public resources, especially rates, were increasing rapidly with the growth in size of the city and Barnett advocates some 'municipal socialism', i.e. municipally owned essential services such as water, gas and trams which could be run at a profit. Private philanthrophy, in the form of philanthropic and charitable agencies, Barnett estimates, provided an income of £150,000 a year. The point he wants to make, as loudly and clearly as possible, is that there is no lack of resources, only a lack of centralized control and good management. Lack of efficiency, not the poverty of the masses, was the reason why Bristol remained so far away from being the Ideal City.

Barnett's vision of the Ideal City was the outcome of his belief in what he termed 'practicable socialism'. Economic inequalities had always existed and would probably always do so in the future. Even the great wealth produced by the Industrial Revolution had been most unequally shared. Yet it had brought the mass of the population much nearer to acquiring the basic needs of life: food, clothing and shelter. The problem of the future was thus not poverty but luxury. The enjoyment of luxury was the key issue for social justice. Facing this challenge, Barnett tried to define in *The Ideal City* what made life fruitful and pleasant for the individual.

In his article 'Practicable Socialism' (1883) he wrote: 'I can conceive a great change in the condition of the people, worked out in our own generation, without any revolution or break with the past. With wages at their present rate, I can yet imagine the houses made strong and healthy, education and public baths made free, and the possibility of investing in land made easy. I can imagine that, without increase of their private wealth, the poor might have, in libraries, music-halls, and flower gardens that on which wealth

is spent. I can imagine the youth of the nation made strong by
means of fresh air and the doctor's care, the aged made restful by
means of honourable pensions. . . all this I can imagine, because it
is practicable.' *The Ideal City* was Barnett's blue-print of how this
vision could be achieved in one city, Bristol. Yet he hoped it would
be adopted by all cities in due course, and that the sum total of this
effort would create one of the greatest civilizations in the history
of man.

THE IDEAL CITY

Cities increase, and the country becomes more and more empty. Observers shake their heads as they walk through the long, dull streets, and breathe the close air, and see the pale faces of the people. "God," they repeat, "made the country, man made the town." Their hearts sink at the thought of the future, and they find themselves saying that "cities will crowd in a blacker, incessanter line;" that "the din will be more," "the trade denser," and that they will "never see an ennobling sight, or drink of the feeling of quiet, again."

They forget that the highest possible life for men may be a city life; and that the prophets foresaw, not a paradise or a garden, |4| but a city with its streets and its markets, its manifold interests and its hum of life. A man often does well, as David, to leave the sheep folds to come down to see the battle.

We are on the line of progress as we gather in from the country districts, and by common action build up a common home. The activities of the street, of the shop, and of the town meeting, are for many characters the best preparation for life in the City of God.

We have as our neighbours in a city, not the trees and the beasts, but fellow human beings. We can from them learn greater lessons, and with them do greater deeds. We can become more human.

The country may still be best for some people; it is probably at some periods of their lives best for all,—there is an ideal village as there is an ideal city—but the movement of men is obviously from country to city; we must, as a consequence, fashion our cities after the highest pattern. We must make them good for the health as for the wealth of the citizens.

My object is to put before you a pattern, an IDEAL CITY, which is not beyond your reach.

The IDEAL CITY will be large, with a quarter or half a million citizens. There will thus be room for a great variety of life and pursuits. The citizens will find at their own doors the interest that comes from the clash of many thoughts and many experiences. They will have no need to go to London to be awakened to the new dangers, the new pleasures, or the new questions of the time. Because, too, the city is large, every citizen will have a greater sense of responsibility. He will feel himself a citizen of no mean city, and as such he will act, and as such expect to be treated.

The IDEAL CITY will be a seaport, from which ships come and go to foreign parts. The talk of the citizens will thus be of things |6| outside their own interests: they will hear of other ways of living, and of other ways of pleasure, and their minds will grow wider. Their imagination will kindle when they stand on the bridges, and their thoughts follow the stream as it passes onwards to the sea where, a few miles distant in storm and in wind, men struggle and strain in strenuous contest; or cross the ocean to new countries where Englishmen are carving an Empire out of forests and deserts. A city which is near the sea may have more responsibilities, and a greater need of religion and government to curb a sailor population; but it is likely to have more liberty of thought, more poetry, and more adventure among its citizens.

The IDEAL CITY will be within sight of the hills. The poets have, in all times, looked to the hills for help, and not in vain. The citizens who have hills in their neighbourhood are drawn to think of the other side, |7| and to dream of things which they make into pictures as did men of the Italian cities. They are drawn also, in a more practical way, to make excursions to the country, and get a knowledge of Nature. By their visits and in their holidays, they develop a fondness for its beauty, which is the basis of the best sort of patriotism.

The IDEAL CITY will be old, the growth of centuries, bearing on its face the mark of many storms and triumphs. There will be buildings in use which were founded when Englishmen were subject to their Norman conquerors. There will be the very marks left by men of old time, as they hammered out their rough thoughts. Some of their buildings will tell of times of luxury and victory; and in out-of-the-way places there will be remnants of castles and forts where the men of old fought and died for the city's liberties. The citizen as he walks the streets |8| of the IDEAL CITY, notes the odd names, turns by some strange twist, or catches sight of some tower, will feel himself encompassed by a cloud of witnesses, and will hear a voice telling him that the ground he treads is made holy by the toil of the city's fathers.   He will be both humbled and inspired: two conditions necessary to satisfaction.

The IDEAL CITY will be new.   Gone are now the close alleys in which men and children die before their time.   Gone are the houses in which families swarm, and foster a pestilence.   Gone are the smells, the filth, and the danger.   Gone are the old school houses with their babel of sounds from classes all taught in one room. Gone are the cemeteries, which under the quiet shelter of their trees hide the seeds of terrible scourges.   Gone are the workhouses, with their stone-breaking and their deterrent systems.   Gone are the prisons, with their vindictive and hope- |9| killing punishments. Gone are the slaughter-houses, with their ugly and demoralising sights.   The IDEAL CITY will be a new city.   Its streets will be broad and lighted with electric light.   Its houses will be good, fitted with water and warmth for the comfort and the health of its inhabitants.   Its spaces will be many; great open spaces for games; small open spaces, within the reach of every house, for the rest of the week.   Its public buildings will be of many styles, expressive of the character of their uses.

There will be the cathedral brooding over the city, gathering together, as it were, its various interests, its manifold activities, to lift them up to higher issues, to God's uses.   There will be the churches and the chapels, with open doors, offering the chance of quiet, and provoking thought by pictures and music.   There will be the churches and schools, with classrooms and playgrounds: technical schools, |10| commercial schools, high schools.   There will be the University College, with its laboratories, its great hall, and its class-rooms.   There will be the Municipal Offices, with its Town Hall, on which panels an artist will have painted scenes from the city's history, and where the citizens will throng in their thousands to hear great speeches or to listen to great music.

Halls, galleries, libraries, baths, hospitals, colleges, asylums, prisons (many of them brilliant with mosaic) will catch and raise the thoughts of men, as in old days the thoughts of their citizens were caught by the public buildings of Florence or Venice.

The city will extend far and wide, but the air will be so clear that no quarter will be unhealthy on account of smoke, and the tram service will be so complete that no quarter will be isolated. Trees and flowers will grow in the streets along which will run streams |11| of pure water. The traffic will pass over noiseless pavements, and the heart of the city will be as pleasant for residence as the suburb. A walk will be no hardship, because the shop windows will be so arranged as to make pictures in the streets, and the advertisements will be under the control of an artist.

A visitor to the IDEAL CITY would be charmed by its first aspect: its variety of architecture, its beauty of colour, its freshness and purity. He would miss little of what he had left in the country. He would breathe easily, enjoy the play of change, and taste the quiet which comes of deeper feeling. And he would know none of the depression caused by great wealth or great poverty. In the IDEAL CITY none will be very rich, and none will be very poor.

Great wealth is often the sign of vulgar ignorance. Its owners know so little that they find excitement in ostentation, in making |12| a greater show than their neighbours, and in leaving bigger fortunes. They think they are worth what they have.

The passion for wealth is a new thing: it has grown up with a century which has brought new forms of pleasure within men's reach. Children when they are first turned into a field of flowers greedily gather, and strive to carry off, the biggest bunch. Afterwards they learn to pluck delicately, to avoid injury, and to choose well; and when they get to be men and women, they find the greatest pleasure in looking at the field tossing with its glowing colours.

People scramble for the wealth which modern discovery has opened up, as the children try to get the biggest bunch of flowers from the field they first know. It is simply a mark of ignorance, and, like that of the children, it will pass away. Already there is more refinement in pleasure, and by-and-by people will see it is better to enjoy in common than in private.

|13| In our IDEAL CITY people will have been educated to find interest in knowledge and beauty. They will have learnt that sufficient excitement is to be found in massing up knowledge of how men think, live, and act, and in creating higher and higher forms of beauty. They will be too refined to parade their superiority by building big houses, adding hothouse to hothouse, carriage to

carriage; too refined to wish, after their death, to be called "mil-lionaires." They will also, if religious teachers do their duty, be too Christ-like to wish to keep for themselves what might be used for others—to spend on luxury what others need for food.

Personally, I believe that the life of any city depends on the religious sense of its individuals. It is the realisation of God's presence as the Righteous and the Loving which strengthens men to dare to be their best, and makes them masters of circum- |14| stances. But here I am trying to trace possible changes in outward things, and their effect on the happiness and character of people. Life is more than its environment, but its environment does influence life.

In the IDEAL CITY there will be no great wealth, because education will have made wealth seem vulgar, and because pride in their city will make the wealthy more anxious to decorate it than them-selves. They who have money will spend it on the city for the citizens' good. They will lay out open spaces, raise and decorate their public buildings. They will endow the bands which play in the parks and the halls. They will employ the artists who will make the streets a very gallery of pictures. They will do this, and they themselves will live simple lives, enjoying to the full the good gifts of the age, but rousing no strife nor anger by their selfishness, vulgarity, or ostentation.

|15| Great poverty will also be absent, because great poverty is a sign of neglect. The very poor are with us, to a large extent, *because* someone has erred; *because* schools are inefficient or the children are let play truant; *because* drink-shops are so frequent; *because* the weak have not been helped, and the wilful have not been trained; *because* the health of the people has been broken by ill-drained houses, smoke-laden air, and impure or insufficient water; *because* the poor have not had care in the time of sickness, nor education in the time of ignorance, nor love in the time of temptation and need. Great poverty is largely due to someone's neglect.

Most people who are poor need not, indeed, be so poor as they are. They have done what they ought not to have done, and none can rise except by their own effort; but I repeat that great poverty is largely due to someone's neglect.

|16| In our IDEAL CITY there will be no such neglect. Knowledge and goodwill will join together to give to every child the best

education, and to secure its use of the gift; to render every house
and street as healthy as the healthiest hillside in the world; to
provide the best doctor and the most comfortable hospital for
everyone who is sick; and to have at hand a friend for everyone in
trouble.   In our IDEAL CITY a good Government, inspired by religion—by a religion which puts right and love before the claims of
denominations,—will see that none of its children perish for want
of health, knowledge, or care.   If there are those who resist, these
it will restrain and in its prisons give them the discipline which is
good.   Neglect is often more evident in the absence of chastisement
than in the absence of care.

Great wealth among the few and great poverty among the many
make an atmosphere |17| in which Art cannot live.   Bishop Westcott
has said: "When Greek Art was greatest, it was consecrated to
public use; and one chief danger of modern Society is, lest the growth
of private wealth should lead to the diversion of the highest artistic
power from the common service."   And another writer has truly
said: "Art is never exotic, to be nourished delicately by a few and
kept from contact with the world."

In our IDEAL CITY Art will grow out of common life, undisturbed
by contrasts of wealth and poverty.   The people will have pleasure
in their work, and leisure to admire what is beautiful.

Our visitor would, therefore, escape the depression so often caused
in great cities by the contrasts of great wealth and great poverty;
and because vice so often follows on self-indulgence or despair, he
would see fewer of those sights which make the heart of man sick.
He would not meet the ragged children selling papers and matches;
nor see the |18| streets, in the evening, crowded with boys and girls
too ignorant to have an object to seek, or an interest to talk
about—an aimless crowd waiting to do mischief.   He would not
find his fellow-creatures, emaciated by want or disease sleeping on
steps trodden daily by their rich owners; he would not meet the
drunken, lawless crowd as it leaves the wretched drinking shops; he
would not see women, in the likeness of his mother or sister, offering
themselves on the streets, being in hell without knowing it.

And yet the absence of contrast would not mean monotony, the
visitor would find everywhere signs of varied life and varied occupation.   His mind would be kept active as it leaped from face to
face, from the dresses to the merchandise stored on the quays, or

as it tried to keep pace with the moving panorama.   At one moment
a factory or a ship would be pouring out a crowd of workmen,
stained |19| with the dust of their pursuit; at another, from a market
would flow a mingled crowd of customers and country men; on the
pavements, merchants, clerks, students, officials, foreigners, sailors,
workwomen, housewives, would all be hurrying or talking.   He
would see, perhaps, a civic procession, headed by its trumpeters—the
Major and Corporation in their robes, with sword-bearer and main-
tenance cap.   They are returning from the Cathedral, where they
have just offered service, and listened to a sermon from one of the
great preachers of the day.   Then he would come across a procession
of trade unionists, or friendly society men, demonstrating with
bands and banners their delight in their strength.   They are hardly
out of sight when he would see the co-operators gathering outside
their hall, where they have been discussing a plan to advance
municipal government to a higher stage; while just |20| opposite
would be the merchants debating the effect of the last treaty.   Later
in the day our visitor would find party after party preparing either
for an excursion to the country, or gathering at the doors of concert
halls and theatres.   By road, by river, or by rail, thousands would
be passing out to the quiet and beauty of Nature; while others
would, by the help of music and acting, or by the words of teachers,
be passing out to the even larger world of thought.

If our visitor became a resident, he would find that experience
in no way belied his first impression.   He would be stirred to new
activities as he talked with men who had travelled and read, and
entered with them into hopes of even better times.   He would be
carried into heights and depths of feeling as by contact he learnt
more of the joys and sorrows of humanity.   He would find in the
daily papers a literature offering to him a |21| ground for admiration,
hope and love; articles taking a wide view of progress; notices of
books; and tales—not of horrors, but of heroisms.   He would
become conscious of his grandeur as, in association with others, he
found himself labouring to make his city more helpful, more beautiful, nearer his ideal of the City of God.   No citizen in the IDEAL
CITY would be dull.

Such, in halting words, is the outline of the pattern city.   The ideal
is not impracticable; it is not out of reach; it does not depend on

a changed human nature, nor on a social revolution.   Bristol could
be made after this pattern.   Our city lies among the hills and near
the sea.   It has a past rich in memories and great deeds; its streets
and its buildings are full of voices; its citizens have been patriots,
poets and adventurers.   Are not its merchants known to this day
as "venturers"? |22| Have we not schools and charities endowed by
those whose interest was in their city, not in their wills, their
carriages, their gardens, or their houses?   Are we not encompassed
by memories?   Have we not among us children of Cabot, Canynge,
Colston, Thorne, Carr and Mary Carpenter?

Is not Bristol, thanks to its able medical officers and its position,
one of the healthiest of towns?   Is it not one of the most beautiful
and the most interesting?   Bristol could be all I have pictured.
It is growing.   Great are the changes since my boyhood.   The
streets are cleaner and wider; the houses are better, the schools more
fit.   It has a magnificent technical college; the beginning of a
University college; a grammar school of repute; well-stored libraries;
and some swimming baths.   Yet Bristol is not what a city might
be: it is far behind other cities smaller and less endowed than itself.
|23| Bristol could be all I have pictured: and yet a picture such as
I have painted is almost a satire on the squalid lanes and courts;
the mean public buildings; the back-to-back houses; the lawless,
ignorant crowds; the smoke-laden air; the wealth which hardens,
and the poverty which degrades.

A list of the powers in the hands of the Councils and Boards is
eloquent as to what is possible and as to what has been neglected.

I. The Town Council, by the application of the Artizans' Dwelling
Act, could replace unfit dwellings by fit.

It could compel factories to consume their own smoke.

It could provide a crematorium.

It could make its buildings ennobling and inspiring.

It could by cheap and new tram lines make more of the hills
available for residences, and repay itself out of their rent.
|24| It could secure that all food and drink should be pure.

It could complete the sewerage system, and make the river sweet
even in the hottest months.

It could inspect, regulate, and provide lodging-houses, so that no
wayfarer should ever suffer from dirt or vice which order would
prevent.

It could establish an art gallery.

It could open the libraries and museums on Sundays.

It could suppress improper houses.

It could make playgrounds.

It might be a model employer.

It could increase and develop the means for washing and bathing.

It might increase its lighting and decrease its police rate.

II. The School-board could interest the children's minds and make school attractive.

|25| It could make children handy by manual work, and train them in drawing and practical exercises.

It could provide playgrounds large enough for games at every school.

It could, at Central Schools, continue education until the children reached the age of 14 or 15.

III. The Board of Guardians might organise a pension system.

It might make its workhouse a training school for the training of the unemployed.

It might make its Infirmary a hospital, and bring comforts within the reach of every sick person.

IV. The Magistrates might control the drink shops, of which there is at present one to every 193 persons.

The expense involved in such changes is not a necessary obstacle. The Japanese have made far greater changes. Fifty years |26| ago their ways and government were behind those of England in the time of Queen Elizabeth, and now they are, at least, on a level with modern times. They have established an army, a navy, a school system, and they have not imposed so heavy a burden on the people as is borne by Bristolians.

Good management can accomplish what seems to be a miracle. It is "in a wife," and not "with a wife," that a fortune is found. It is in the heads of the rulers, and not in the pockets of taxpayers, that enough money may be found to make the city desirable to live in.

Bristol has abundant resources. (1) The rateable value of the city proper increased in twenty years from £256,000 to £383,000, *i.e.* 50 per cent.

(2) The public estate of the city brings in over £30,000 a year, and increases year by year.

|27| (3) The profits on water, gas and trams, if they had been started and worked by the city, would have brought in £50,000 a year.   If their services were bought, even at the present prices, a profit may be secured.

(4) The rateable value of the whole city, on which rates may be levied, is over £1,000,000.

Bristol has had and has generous citizens.   Its charities are said to amount to £150,000 a year, and its men and its women are notorious for the interest they have in what is honest, of good report, and helpful.   At the present time there are many citizens working quietly in Bristol for the good of others, whose example gives the lie to those who rail at employers, landlords, and ladies, as if all were selfish.   Bristol, by its history, its position, its great names, has a way of evoking loyalty, and Bristol men are so fond of their city that they include its abuses and |28| resent the stranger who suggests their removal.

Bristol, in its accumulated wealth, in its rich citizens, and, in its army of men and women living simple and devoted lives, has ample resources.   One thing necessary is the good management which would introduce unity into the system.   Good management could make the resources of Bristol do for Bristol what smaller resources have done for other towns.   It would not be hard to present a model budget, and it would be good practice for young reformers to draw up and publish such a budget.

But why are these things so?   Bristol citizens have not cared for the city government.   At the last election of the Town Council only 10,036 voted out of an electorate of 33,307 as there were no contests in seven wards.   At the last School Board election only 11,932 voted out of an electorate of 33,307.

|29| The citizens may be generous—they may care for others; they give, as we know, to societies, to churches, to relieve the poor,—but they have not cared, as Thorne, Carr, and many others cared, to strengthen the city government.   All these gave their money to the Mayor and Corporation, but lately there have been no great gifts of parks or picture-galleries; no great bequests putting power into the hands of the Boards to lighten the burden of the rates.   The rich, very often refuse high office; and the workmen will not give the penny a week which would enable their representatives on the Council or Boards to sit and work without anxiety.

The citizens may be fond of their city, but somehow they do not care for its government. They fail for want of imagination and that unresisting energy which imagination provokes. Where an idea reigns a way will be |30| found. Ideas are stronger than indolence, stronger than greed. If Bristolians imagined the possible, it would soon be the actual.

Mr. Bryce has said that the one conspicuous failure of the United States "is its government of cities." That failure is due to the citizens' absorption in their own interests. Each is for himself—each striving to get on, to amass money, and to get comforts. The rich hurry off to their suburban haunts, from which they keep out the poor. The poor strive to become rich and do likewise. Americans have no ideal of city life.

In one of the Cobden Club essays it is said: "A true municipality should completely grasp the life of the community, and in doing so should aim at expressing the communal idea, 'One for all, all for one.'"

In another part of the same essay it is said: "The work of a town should be done with such completeness as to leave no sort of |31| danger or evil unchecked, no material defect uncured, no intellectual want uncared for. It should be done with such regularity of method as to ensure the steady and easy working of the complex machine; with such stateliness of manner as to dignify the corporate life; with such a spirit of earnestness and thoroughness and self-sacrifice as to raise the general tone and standard of public service to the highest level; and with such unity of feeling as to bind all classes together with a real sense of belonging to a community worthy of being served, honoured, and obeyed."

This will not be possible until citizens are captured by the thought of what their city might be; until by love, by hope, by interest their powers are drawn out to use the means in their hands to create a city which shall be a joy in the earth; until they give their time and their money to |32| make Councils and Boards keen for its beauty and its health.

Our duty is clear. We have to preach the coming of the IDEAL CITY; to open the eyes of citizens to see what is possible; to show them, lying here, amid the hills and by the river, a city where there shall be nothing to offend, everything to help. We have to preach "Bristol as it might be," and to arouse every elector, every citizen,

to do his part in preparing the way.   It is not money that is lacking
to turn "Bristol as it is" into "Bristol as it might be," it is ideas.

NOTE TO CIVICS: AS APPLIED SOCIOLOGY
PARTS I AND II

The aim of Geddes's two papers was to offer an introduction to his
concept of civics, and a methodology to guide others interested in
solving urban problems. What he wanted above all was to encourage
people to study cities, not in a fragmented fashion such as pursuing
specific urban problems, but in a comprehensive manner, encom-
passing the city as a whole. Such an approach had to be based on
science and art, since it could only be built up from observations,
made in a systematic manner, and interpreted by recourse to cultural
criteria. The two together, scientific fact and artistic understanding,
made up the elements which constituted the art of civics. Such a
subject, formed from disparate elements, could only be given shape
in a practical context and Geddes put forward the social survey as
the ideal way of pursuing the subject. The purpose of the whole
exercise was to awaken new responses to urbanization and its social
consequences. The social survey was to be followed by social service
and this is what made civics a subject of applied sociology.

Objections to this generalist approach, on the grounds that Geddes
was ignoring political, economic and historical realities, were made
quite forcefully in the discussions following his paper, reprinted in
full here. Geddes, however, felt confident enough to ignore them as
he believed that fundamentally, the most important knowledge
required by the student of cities was that provided by the natural
sciences and the concept of evolution. Further, the application of
biological insight into the social conditions of man demanded new
ways of thinking in which conventional responses, with their
emphasis on politics and economics, were irrelevant. He was thus
beyond the reach of criticism from his contemporaries. However,
he was able to impress some by his unerring instinct for the weak
links in the social and economic theories of others; and he was at

67

his most convincing in his strong support of those scientific endeavours which could be made to serve man. He was constantly
encouraging others not to be afraid of science and to see what
benefits chemistry had brought to agriculture, and biology to
medicine. His objective in establishing 'civics' was to dispel fear of
cities and mass urbanization, and to release the creative responses
of individuals towards solving modern urban problems.

One of the most important contributions of his first paper was
thus simply the optimism Geddes conveyed that the problems of
cities could be mastered, and that it was only a matter of finding
the best way of doing it. He believed the best method was to look
at the geographical location of a city, the evolution of its historical
traditions, economic, social and cultural, and the development of
present-day citizens, especially their education. This was the evolutionary scientists' approach to an analysis of environment and
organism. It provided Geddes with a starting point for studying
cities and social problems quite outside contemporary concerns
about poverty, housing and slum clearance, public health etc. The
results of other social survey work such as that of Charles Booth
and Seebohm Rowntree had established the gigantic proportions of
these problems, and had highlighted the fact that without a massive
re-allocation of resources, which was politically impossible at this
time, they could not be solved. Geddes was convinced this was the
wrong way to look at cities and their social problems, and his first
paper was devoted to trying to change people's viewpoint.

The right way to look at cities, he suggested, was to establish the
city in its specific physical context and then to explore the causes
of progress and decay of environment and organism. The starting
point was thus the city in its region. The stressing of geographical
factors in relation to the understanding of cities and city life was
one of Geddes's most important contributions. His concern for
defining those factors which directly influenced urban life made him
concentrate on the region, as he did not see city life as something
divorced from the countryside. What he sought was a geographical
unit which would provide a satisfactory microcosm of society as a
whole – the urban and rural together. The unit he invented was the
Valley section, a cross-section of the region following a river from
its source in the hills to its mouth at the sea, and the significance

of this unit was that it could be generally applied to most cities, located on rivers, in any country in the world. Above all, it could be used to delimit the extent of Geddes's social surveys which were aimed not at specific problems in urban areas, like Booth's study of poverty in the East End of London, but at the city in its geographical region.

What he was striving for in his own words was 'the elemental and naturalist-like point of view even in the greatest cities'. Geddes always made much of the contrast between the 'urban' and 'rural' response to cities and he strongly identified himself with the latter. He believed that the countryman was able to observe the strange social and cultural milieu of the city with a keener eye, since his pre-conceived 'norms' were not shaped by the experience of urban life. He argued that in spite of all the nineteenth-century developments towards city-planning, 'we are still building from our inherited instincts like bees'. To persuade people to shift from this to a rational scientific development of our cities, which would lead ultimately to the elimination of social problems, was the major difficulty. What was needed was a better understanding of the forces shaping the city. He tried to construct in his Regional Survey, techniques for determining how the past had led to the present. What he developed was a historical model of evolution.

History was thus 'a drama in time', moving from one stage of evolution to another. Geddes's purpose here was to awaken a new consciousness that all cities, even those most transformed by the Industrial Revolution, had a past, and that this past was incorporated in a physical and cultural legacy which was of vital importance in the present. His favourite illustration of this theme was Edinburgh, where he had developed his ideas of the Regional Survey and which furnished him with the best examples, in buildings and layout, of the importance of the past in the present. He considered he now had the two key elements for an evolutionary study, an understanding of the physical environment through a geographical study of the region, and an understanding of those elements of the past which had shaped the present. The challenge was the future.

In his first paper Geddes hardly tried to meet this challenge. He confined himself to a few comments about the need to study the citizen in the process of development, and to be self-conscious about

future development. This was what he meant by his grand phrases
advocating 'the growth of civic consciousness and conscience' and
'the awakening of citizenship toward civic renascence'. The vague-
ness of his concepts was the main criticism put forward in the
discussion of his paper and earned him the comment from Charles
Booth that he had expected Geddes to be more practical as he had
just been engaged on an actual project, the plan for Dunfermline.
Geddes's second paper was thus an attempt, on his part, to define
his subject more precisely. His arguments, however, proved to be
even more unexpected.

In his second paper Geddes wanted to convince his audience that
civics was a subject with the practical objective of leading students
of civics towards accurate forecasting of the future. Geddes really
believed this was possible though the chances of success depended
on two factors. First, an understanding of the present evolution of
cities; and secondly, a keen perception of those factors in the present,
the 'buds' discernable only to the trained eye, which were going to
influence the future. To arrive at the former, Geddes set out to
establish a general approach for analysing the evolution of cities.
In spite of his great commitment to geography and the importance
of the environment, he did not fall into the trap of geographical
determinism. Instead he tried to develop some general sociological
categories to fit into his established environmental model, the Valley
section. He took the basic Le Play formula of society – Place, Work,
Folk – and constructed from it a method for analysing the city.
This method of notation was, however, merely a shorthand for the
range of material relevant to the 'bud' hunter. The terminology
Place, Work, Folk, covered geography, economics, anthropology,
nature – Geddes's argument being that all knowledge touching on
the human condition needs to be encompassed by the student of
evolution.

If this was the case, however, the problem was utilizing a wide
range of knowledge in a specific context, both to understand the
evolution of the past to the present, and to determine the needs and
direction for the future. Geddes provided an ingenious way out of
this difficulty by sticking to what he believed was the 'biological'
viewpoint and developing his notations. In the centre of the stage
was man, an organism with physical and psychic properties. Modern

man was a product of those elements of organic continuity, built
up between generations. He had at once an inheritance which was
organic and psychic, and a heritage which encompassed economic
wealth and social and cultural traditions. Starting from here, Geddes
constructed a composite model, step by step, under general headings,
referring to those factors he believed had most influence on man's
inheritance and heritage. His steps were uncertain and certainly he
managed to confuse his audience.

Yet the main thrust of his argument does emerge from all the
sub-sections he used to make his case. Social problems in the city
cannot be solved with reference to specific factors such as low wages
or bad housing. Economic activity, occupations and locations are
only part of the picture. Of equal importance are biological units
such as the family and social and cultural traditions which provide
the basis from which man learns to adapt to technological change.
The evils of the city such as disease, vice and crime are not just
problems, they are the result of this process of adaptability being
allowed to go on without direction or control. To solve them the
whole social life of the city has to be directed towards higher
evolutionary goals. Yet selfconscious effort to achieve progressive
evolutionary trends can only come about if all citizens are united.
Students of civics (or Geddes himself, for instance, in his plan for
Dunfermline) could point in the right direction, but evolutionary
progress could only come from within each and every organism.

What Geddes therefore wanted was to encourage in the present
and future a society whose main concern was the nurture of its
people. At some stage, the economic and social system had to be
fitted to the people and not vice versa. Geddes felt that the opposite
trend had been taking place since the Industrial Revolution and he
divided the subsequent period up into evolutionary stages. The
Industrial Revolution period itself was the paleotechnic age when
the new science and technology was in its infancy, and men became
so intoxicated with their new powers that humanity was sacrificed
on the altar of economic progress. Then he discerned a neotechnic
age, when technology became more sophicsticated and was harnessed
not only to produce goods but also to lighten labour. What he looked
for in the future was a geotechnic age, when science and technology
could be used to improve the material and physical conditions of

the people, and finally a eugenic age, when the whole system would
be devoted to the nurture of people. In that age, man would have
become master of his own destiny and Utopia would be within
reach.

This was the long-term objective which Geddes insisted was
perfectly practical, in view of the rapid development of science and
technology. But it could only be realized if, in the short-term,
students of civics were recruited to seek the most promising 'buds'
for the future, and to ensure their development, by getting a response
from the public at large, through education and propaganda. Geddes
therefore concluded his second paper with a proposal for encouraging
civic exhibitions. The result of a Regional survey was the collection
of a mass of material which could most readily be analysed if hung
as an exhibition. And such an exhibition would generate local
interest and encourage citizens to participate in those kinds of
activities which would lead to social and environmental betterment,
the prerequisite for evolutionary progress. Geddes suggested that
such exhibitions need not be local and regional only, but national
and international, and he noted a number of examples including the
Chicago exposition of 1893, the Paris World Fair of 1900, the St
Louis Exhibition of 1903 which actually had a municipal section,
and the town exhibitions in Germany and elsewhere.

He made an appeal for support, by name, to the Rt. Hon. Charles
Booth, Canon Barnett, and Mr Horsfall, who were amongst his
audience, and the last footnote to the paper suggests that Canon
Barnett had launched the idea of a civic exhibition with success
amongst his Toynbee Hall Residents. Geddes also did not miss an
opportunity for trying to incorporate Mr Francis Galton's subject,
Eugenics, within his own framework for Civics. Galton had come
out of retirement, at the age of 82, to make a plea for the study of
Eugenics as an important element in sociological studies. Galton's
Eugenics and Geddes's Civics were the main attractions of the first
session of the British Sociological Society. Eugenics, the scientific
study of racial improvement, however, became immediately popular
to a much greater extent than civics. Its popular appeal lay in the
fact that ideas concerning the improvement and purity of the race
were fed by deep-seated emotions and irrational prejudices of a
racialist and anti-social nature, widely current in 1904. Anti-sem-

itism and hostility to the lower orders could be united under the guise of a crude, pseudo-scientific social Darwinism, which seemed implicit to the subject of Eugenics.

Geddes saw the danger. J. Arthur Thompson, Professor of Biology at the University of Aberdeen, and a former student of Geddes, was asked to address the Sociological Society to refute such blatantly ignorant adaptations of scientific theory to social life. In his own papers, Geddes spoke of Eugenics as being the whole purpose of his own subject, Civics. The social service which was to be the outcome of the Regional social survey was to be a form of planning for the physical and social well-being of individuals which would lead to an improvement in the social organism, the eugenist objective. Unfortunately for Geddes however, since his main concern was with cities, his own supporters tended to veer to the opposite pole to the eugenists. Crude social Darwinism was replaced by crude environmental determinism. Whilst neither Galton nor Geddes themselves underestimated the problems of developing a 'scientific' approach to sociological data, their use of evolutionary theory bred a false confidence.

The result of Geddes's two papers on civics led to the formation of a Civics Committee of the Sociological Society when the interests of the society split in four different directions. Committees were set up devoted to Eugenics, Civics, Education and Social Economy. The aims of all these committees were to promote informed social action as well as to develop their subjects. Geddes's Civics, however, was not so much a subject as an education. 'Bud' hunting and the direction of social evolution was not an academic subject. The future of cities could not be properly determined by men working at their desks. Even Ebenezer Howard, who was present at Geddes's first lecture, had a 'drawing board' approach to Utopia which, thus, had to be outside the mainstream of the social experience of the masses. Students of civics would be equipped to investigate and advise on the problems of all cities using Geddes's generalized formulae as a guide for future action. The aim was to produce an individual planner, freed from the strait jacket of ideology, confident in his own abilities, and sensitive to the pattern of evolution within which all vital decisions had to be made.

The purpose of Geddes's Civic Exhibitions and Regional Surveys was not to provide a methodology for urban sociology, though he hoped one would emerge after years of experiment and experience. The purpose was to awaken the instincts and to refine the intuitions of a select few who could be made responsible for guiding the direction of the future. A growing consciousness of the need for modern town planning had been developing nationally and internationally. Geddes felt that the potential within this movement would only be realized if the quality of individuals recruited to its service was high, and if they were widely supported. Such individuals could not be bound by the problem-orientated approach of Booth and Rowntree, with the social and administrative approach of Barnett, or with the Eugenist approach of Galton, concentrating on the organism alone. A student of civics could encompass all these and a little more, since the geographical and regional approach covered all aspects of social life. Thus the two papers on 'Civics' were not the basis for a new discipline. They were a blueprint for the training of an urban sociologist whose skills were to be refined by modern knowledge and then put to practical, rather than academic, use.

Geddes's lectures together with discussion, written communications and Press comments, were published for the Sociological Society by Macmillan, in *Sociological Papers 1904* (1905) and *Sociological Papers 1905* (1906).

CIVICS: AS APPLIED SOCIOLOGY

BY PROFESSOR GEDDES

Read before the Sociological Society at a Meeting in the School of Economics and Political Science (University of London), Clare Market, W.C., at 5 p.m., on Monday, July 18th, 1904; the Rt. Hon. CHARLES BOOTH, F.R.S., in the Chair.

INTRODUCTION

This department of sociological studies should evidently be, as far as possible, concrete in treatment.   If it is to appeal to practical men and civic workers, it is important that the methods advocated for the systematic study of cities, and as underlying fruitful action, be not merely the product of the study, but rather be those which may be acquired in course of local observation and practical effort.   My problem is thus to outline such general ideas as may naturally crystallise from the experience of any moderately-travelled observer of varied interests; so that his observation of city after city, now panoramic and impressionist, again detailed, should gradually develop towards an orderly Regional Survey.   This point of view has next to be correlated with the corresponding practical experience, that which may be acquired through some varied experiences of citizenship, and thence rise toward a larger and more orderly conception of civic action—as Regional Service.   In a word, then, Applied Sociology in general, or |104| Civics, as one of its main departments, may be defined as the application of Social Survey to Social Service.

In this complex field of study as in simpler preliminary ones, our everyday experiences and commonsense interpretations gradually become more systematic, that is, begin to assume a scientific character; while our activities, in becoming more orderly and comprehensive, similarly approximate towards art. Thus there is emerging more and more clearly for sociological studies in general, for their concrete fields of application in city after city, the conception of a scientific centre of observation and record on the one hand, and of a corresponding centre of experimental endeavour on the other—in short of Sociological Observatory and Sociological Laboratory, and of these as increasingly co-ordinated. Indeed, is not such association of observations and experiments, are not such institutions actually incipient here and elsewhere? I need not multiply instances of the correlation of science and art, as of chemistry with agriculture, or biology with medicine. Yet, on the strictly sociological plane and in civic application they are as yet less generally evident, though such obvious connections as that of vital statistics with hygienic administration, that of commercial statistics with politics, are becoming recognised by all. In the paper with which this Society's work lately opened, the intimate connection between a scientific demography and a practical eugenics has been clearly set forth. But this study of the community in the aggregate finds its natural parallel and complement in the study of the community as an integrate, with material and immaterial structures and functions, which we call the City. Correspondingly, the improvement of the individuals of the community, which is the aim of eugenics, involves a corresponding civic progress. Using (for the moment at least) a parallel nomenclature, we see that the sociologist is concerned not only with "demography" but with "politography," and that "eugenics" is inseparable from "politogenics." For the struggle for existence, though observed mainly from the side of its individuals by the demographer, is not only an intra-civic but an inter-civic process; and if so, ameliorative selection, now clearly sought for the individuals in detail as eugenics, is inseparable from a corresponding civic art—a literal "Eupolitogenics."

A—THE GEOGRAPHIC SURVEY OF CITIES

Coming to concrete Civic Survey, where shall we begin? Not only in variety and magnitude of civic activities, but, thanks especially to the work of Mr. Charles Booth and his collaborators in actual social survey also, London may naturally claim pre-eminence. Yet even at best, does not this vastest of world cities remain a less or more foggy labyrinth, from which sur- |105| rounding regions with their smaller cities can be but dimly descried, even with the best intentions of avoiding the cheap generalisation of "the provinces"? For our more general and comparative study, then, simpler beginnings are preferable. More suitable, therefore, to our fundamental thesis—that no less definite than the study of races and usages or languages, is that of the groupings of men—is the clearer outlook, the more panoramic view of a definite geographic region, such, for instance, as lies beneath us upon a mountain holiday. Beneath vast hunting desolations lie the pastoral hillsides, below these again scattered arable crofts and sparsely dotted hamlets lead us to the small upland village of the main glen: from this again one descends to the large and prosperous village of the foothills and its railway terminus, where lowland and highland meet. East or west, each mountain valley has its analogous terminal and initial village, upon its fertile fan-shaped slope, and with its corresponding minor market; while, central to the broad agricultural strath with its slow meandering river, stands the prosperous market town, the road and railway junction upon which all the various glen-villages converge. A day's march further down, and at the convergence of several such valleys, stands the larger county-town—in the region before me as I write, one of added importance, since not only well nigh central to Scotland, but as the tidal limit of a till lately navigable river. Finally, at the mouth of its estuary, rises the smoke of a great manufacturing city, a central world-market in its way. Such a river system is, as geographer after geographer has pointed out, the essential unit for the student of cities and civilisations. Hence this simple geographical method of treatment must here be pled for as fundamental to any really orderly and comparative treatment of our subject. By descending from source to sea we follow the development of civilisation from its simple origins to its complex resultants; nor can any element of this be omitted. Were we to begin with the peasant hamlet as our initial unit, and forget the hinterlands of pasture, forest, and chase (an error to which the writer on cities is naturally prone), the anthropologist would soon remind us that in forgetting the hunter, we had omitted the essential germ of active militarism, and hence very largely of aristocratic rule. Similarly, |106| in ignoring the pastoral life, we should be

losing sight of a main fount of spiritual power, and this not only
as regards the historic religions, but all later culture elements also,
from the poetic to the educational.   In short, then, it takes the
whole region to make the city.   As the river carries down contributions from its whole course, so each complex community, as we
descend, is modified by its predecessors.   The converse is no doubt
true also, but commonly in less degree.

In this way with the geographer we may rapidly review and
extend our knowledge of the grouping of cities.   Such a survey of
a series of our own river-basins, say from Dee to Thames, and of
a few leading Continental ones, say the Rhine and Meuse, the Seine
and Loire, the Rhone, the Po, the Danube—and, if possible, in
America also, at least the Hudson and Mississippi—will be found
the soundest of introductions to the study of cities.   The comparison
of corresponding types at once yields the conviction of broad general
unity of development, structure, and function.   Thus, with Met-
schnikoff we recognise the succession of potamic, thalassic, and
oceanic civilisations; with Reclus we see the regular distribution of
minor and major towns to have been largely influenced not only by
geographical position but by convenient journey distances.   Again,
we note how the exigencies of defence and of government, the
developments of religion, despite all historic diversities, have been
fundamentally the same.   It is not, of course, to be forgotten how
government, commerce, communications, have concentrated, altered
or at least disguised the fundamental geographical simplicity of this
descending hierarchy from mountain-hamlet to ocean-metropolis;
but it is useful for the student constantly to recover the elemental
and naturalist-like point of view even in the greatest cities.   At
times we all see London as still fundamentally an agglomeration of
villages, with their surviving patches of common, around a mediaeval seaport; or we discern even in the utmost magnificence of Paris,
say its Place de l'Etoile, with its spread of boulevards, but the
hunter's tryst by the fallen tree, with its radiating forest-rides, each
literally arrow-straight.   So the narrow rectangular network of an
American city is explicable only by the unthinking persistence of
the peasant thrift, which grudges good land to road- |107| way, and
is jealous of oblique short cuts.   In short, then, in what seems our
most studied city planning, we are still building from our inherited

instincts like the bees.   Our Civics is thus still far from an Applied
Sociology.

B—THE HISTORIC SURVEY OF CITIES

But a city is more than a place in space, it is a drama in time.
Though the claim of geography be fundamental our interest in the
history of the city is supremely greater; it is obviously no mere
geographic circumstances which developed one hill-fort in Judea,
and another in Attica, into world centres, to this day more deeply
influential and significant than are the vastest modern capitals.
This very wealth of historical interests and resources, the corresponding multiplicity of specialisms, more than ever proves the need
of some means by which to group and classify them.   Some
panoramic simplification of our ideas of history comparable to that
of our geography, and if possible congruent with this, is plainly
what we want.   Again the answer comes through geography,
though no longer in mere map or relief, but now in vertical
section—in the order of strata ascending from past to present,
whether we study rock-formations with the geologist, excavate
more recent accumulations with the archaeologist, or interpret ruins
or monuments with the historian.   Though the primitive conditions
we have above noted with the physiographer remain apparent,
indeed usually permanent, cities have none the less their characteristic phases of historic development decipherably superposed.
Thus below even the characteristically patriarchal civilisations, an
earlier matriarchal order is often becoming disclosed.   Our interest
in exploring some stately modern or Renaissance city is constantly
varied by finding some picturesque mediaeval remnant; below this
some fragment of Roman ruin; below this it may be some barbarian
fort or mound.   Hence the fascinating interest of travel, which
compels us ever to begin our survey anew.   Starting with the same
river-basin as before, the geographic panorama now gains a new
and deeper interest.   Primitive centres long forgotten start into
life; pre-historic tumuli give up their dead; to the stone circles the
|108| worshippers return; the British and the Roman camps again
fill with armed men, and beside the prosaic market town arises a
shadowy Arthurian capital.   Next, some moment-centuries later,
a usurper's tower rises and falls; the mediaeval abbey, the great
castles, have their day; with the Reformation and the Renaissance

the towns again are transformed; and yet more thoroughly than ever by the Industrial Revolution, with its factories, railways, steamships, and all that they bring with them.   Thus, for instance, almost more important than the internal transformation and concentration wrought by railway and telegraph, is the selection, amidst the almost innumerable seaports of the older order, of the very few adapted to the deep draught of modern ships.   In a word, not only does the main series of active cities display traces of all the past phases of evolution, but beside this lie fossils, or linger survivals, of almost every preceding phase.

Hence, after many years of experiment and practice in teaching sociology I still find no better method available than that of regional survey, historical as well as geographical.   Beginning with some popular excursion of obvious beauty and romantic interest like that to Melrose, we see with every tourist how naturally and fully the atmosphere and tradition of the Border found its expression and world influence in Sir Walter Scott.   Thence, passing by way of contrast through the long isolated peninsula of Fife, say to representative towns like Kirkcaldy and Largo, we still see the conditions of that individualism of which Adam Smith and Alexander Selkirk ("Robinson Crusoe") have each in his way become the very prototypes.   In such ways the connection of regional geography, history, and social psychology becomes increasingly clear.   Again, we explore the other old Fife seaports, a series of survivals like those of the Zuyder Zee, or again work out in the field the significance of Stirling, so often the strategic centre of Scotland.   Again, Dunfermline, as early mediaeval capital and abbey, furnishes a convenient object lesson preparatory to the study of the larger Edinburgh.   Here, again, its triple centre, in the port of Leith, the Royal Castle, the Abbey of Holyrood, are the respective analogues of the port of London, the Tower, and Westminster; while each city-group has its outlying circle of minor burghs, tardily and imperfectly incorporated into a civic whole.   Again, such a marked contrast of civic origins and developments as those of Glasgow and Edinburgh has to be accounted for; and thus through such progessively complexer surveys we reach the plane of modern civic problems and policies.   Understanding the present as the development of the past, are we not preparing also to understand the future as the development of the present?

The impressiveness of the aspect of Edinburgh to its visitors is thus not |109| merely pictorial. Be the spectator conscious of this or no, it turns primarily upon the contrast of the mediaeval hill-city with its castle ramparts, its fretted cathedral crown, with park and boulevard, with shops, hotels and railway stations. But the historic panorama is unusually complete. See the hill-fort defended by lake and forest, becoming "*castrum puellarum*," becoming a Roman and an Arthurian citadel, a mediaeval stronghold of innumerable sieges, a centre of autocratic and military dictatures, oligarchic governments, at length a museum of the past. So in the city itself. Here the narrow ridge crowded into a single street all the essential organs of a capital, and still presents with the rarest completeness of concentration a conspectus of modern civic life and development; and this alike as regards both spiritual and temporal powers, using these terms in their broadest senses as the respective expressions of the material order and its immaterial counterparts. Thus the royal and noble castles of the Middle Age become with the Renaissance here as everywhere something of palaces, while with the industrial revolution they have become replaced by factories or transformed into breweries. So the guidance of speculative thought, once concentrated in the mediaeval abbey, becomes transferred to the Reformation assembly of divines, to the Renaissance college; and again at the Revolution, is largely taken over by the speculative encyclopædists, of whom Hume and Smith were but the most eminent. Nor are later developments less obvious. Of the following generation, we have the neo-classic architecture which everywhere dominated Europe after the French Revolution and during the First Empire, while of the next generation's reaction against all this in the romantic movement, the neo-Gothic monument of Scott is the most characteristic possible representative. Again, just as in the Oxford movement we had the (appropriately regional) renascence of the idealism of the Cavaliers, so in Edinburgh we have naturally the simultaneous renascence of the Puritan ideal, *e.g.*, in the Free Church, whose monument accordingly rises to dominate the city in its turn. The later period of prosperous Liberalism, the heroic enthusiasms of Empire, have each left their mark; and now in the dominant phase of social evolution, that of Finance, the banks, the financial companies, the press are having their turn as monument builders. Our Old Edinburgh is thus the most condensed example, the visible microcosm of the social evolution which is manifest everywhere; so that as a teaching model of sociological development it may renew its educational attractiveness when its improving hygiene has lessened its medical advantages.

Setting down now these phases of historical development in tabular form, we have a diagram such as the following:—

ANCIENT			RECENT			CONTEMPORARY			INCIPIENT
Primitive	Matri-archal	Patri-archal	Greek and Roman	Mediæval	Renaissance	Revolution	Empire	Finance	? ? ?

which, were it placed erect, we might now compare to the increasing |110| nodes of a growing stem, or rather say the layers of a coral reef, in which each generation constructs its characteristic stony skeleton as a contribution to the growing yet dying and wearying whole. I have elaborated this example of the panoramic aspect of Old Edinburgh as a widely familiar instance of the method of literal survey with which social and civic studies may so conveniently begin; and I press the value of extending these even to the utmost elaborateness of photographic survey: in my view, indeed, a sociological society has at least as much use for a collection of maps, plans and photographs as of statistics, indeed scarcely less than one of books. Of course, in all this I am but recalling what every tourist in some measure knows; yet his impressions and recollections can become an orderly politography, only as he sees each city in terms of its characteristic social formations, and as he utilises the best examples from each phase towards building up a complete picture of the greatest products of civic evolution, temporal and spiritual, of all places and times up to the present. Such a parallel of the historic survey of the city to that of its underlying geological area is thus in no wise a metaphoric one, but one which may be worked out upon maps sections and diagrams almost completely in the same way—in fact, with little change save that of colours and vertical scale. The attempt to express the characteristic and essential life and thought of a given region in each period upon a series of maps is in fact the best method of understanding the everyday map at which we commonly look so unthinkingly.

Much of the preceding, I am assured, must be most unsatisfactory to those who look at cities only from the standpoint of so many committees dealing with police, water, finance, and so on; or to those who are content to view the magnitude, the wealth and the

population, the industries and the manufactures, of a great city
without considering whence these have come and whither they are
leading; equally unsatisfactory also, I fear, to those to whom civic
dignities and precedence, or the alternations of winning political
colours, appear of prime importance.   I can only hope that some
of these may, on consideration, admit that the points of view I
have endeavoured to outline above may be worth some thought and
study as elementary preliminaries to their own more special and
developed interests; and if the society permit.   I hope to approach
these more closely in a later paper.

|111| The abstract economist or legalist, the moral or political
philosopher may also resent the proposed mode of treatment as an
attempt to materialise sociology by reducing it to concrete terms
alone.   But I would reply that observation, so far from excluding
interpretation, is just the very means of preparing for it.   It is the
observant naturalist, the travelled zoologist and botanist, who later
becomes the productive writer on evolution.   It is the historian
who may best venture on into the philosophy of history;—to think
the reverse is to remain in the pre-scientific order altogether: hence
the construction of systems of abstract and deductive economics,
politics or morals, has really been the last surviving effort of
scholasticism.   Viewed as Science, Civics is that branch of Sociology
which deals with Cities—their origin and distribution; their development and structure; their functioning, internal and external,
material and psychological; their evolution, individual and associated.   Viewed again from the practical side, that of applied science,
Civics must develop through experimental endeavour into the more
and more effective Art of enhancing the life of the city and of
advancing its evolution.   With the first of these lines of study, the
concretely scientific, our philosophical outlook will not fail to widen;
with the second, the practical, our ethical insight will not fail to
deepen also.

As primarily a student of living nature in evolution, I have
naturally approached the city from the side of its geographic and
historic survey, its environment and functional change; yet it is but
a step from these to the abstract interpretations of the economist
or the politician, even of philosopher and moralist.   Again, since
in everyday practice co-ordinating the literal maps of each civic
surveys with even more concretely detailed plans as gardener and

builder, I find less danger than may at first appear of ignoring the
legitimate demands of the needed practical division of labour in the
city's service. When the first mutual unfamiliarity is got over, there
is thus also a greatly diminished distance between speculative
thinkers and practical men, who at present, in this country especially,
stand almost unrelated: the evolutionist student and worker thus
begins to furnish the missing link between them.

C—THE CITIZEN IN PROCESS OF DEVELOPMENT

Leaving now the external survey of the city by help of its material
framework, its characteristic buildings and predominant styles, for
the deeper psychological survey of the citizens themselves, we may
conveniently begin with these also in their process of development—in fact, our method compels us to this course.   We enter
then a school; and if we bring fresh eyes we may soon be agreed
that the extraordinary babel of studies its time-table and curriculum
reveal, is intelligible from no single one of the various |112| geo-
graphic or historic points of view we have traversed from mountain
to sea, or from past to present.   But this unprecedented conflict
of studies becomes at once intelligible when viewed apart from any
and every definite theory of education yet promulgated by educationists, and even acquires a fresh theory of its own—that of the
attempted recapitulation of the survivals of each and all preceding
periods in their practical or speculative aspects, particularly the
later legends and literatures, their rituals and codes.   Thus, the
inordinate specialisation upon arithmetic, the exaggeration of all
three R's, is plainly the survival of the demand for cheap yet
efficient clerks, characteristic of the recent and contemporary financial period.

The ritual of examinations with its correlation of memorising and
muscular drill is similarly a development of the imperial order,
historically borrowed from the Napoleonic one; the chaotic "general
knowledge" is similarly a survival of the encyclopaedic period; that
is, of the French Revolution and the Liberal Movement generally;
the Latin grammar and verses are of course the survivals of the
Renaissance, as the precise fidelity to absurd spelling is the imitation
of its proof readers; the essay is the abridged form of the mediaeval
disputation; and only such genuine sympathy with Virgil or Tacitus,
with Homer or Plato as one in a thousand acquires, is truly Roman

or Greek at all.   The religious instruction, however, re-interpreted
by the mediaeval Church or the Reformation, has still its strength
in some of the best elements of patriarchal literature; while the fairy
tale, by which all this superincumbent weight of learning is sometimes alleviated, is the child's inheritance from the matriarchal
order.   Finally, the apple and the ball, at the bottom of this whole
burden of books, complete the recapitulation; as the one, the raw
fruit; the other, the ready missile, of primeval man.   Our child then
is heir of all the ages more fully than he or his teachers commonly
realise.   The struggle for mastery of the schools is thus no temporary
feud, but an unending battle; one destined to increase rather than
diminish; for in this there is the perpetual clash of all the forces of
good heredity and evil atavism, of all the new variations also,
healthy or diseases.

|113| D–THE APPLIED SOCIOLOGY OF THE PRESENT
The city and its children thus historically present a thoroughly
parallel accumulation of survivals or recapitulations of the past in
the present.   Few types nowadays are pure, that is, keep strictly
to their period; we are all more or less mixed and modernised.   Still,
whether by temporal or spiritual compulsion, whether for the sake
of bread or honour, each mainly and practically stands by his order,
and acts with the social formation he belongs to.   Thus now the
question of the practical civics, that is, of the applied sociology, of
each individual, each body or interests may be broadly defined; it
is to emphasise his particular historic type, his social formation and
influence in the civic whole, if not indeed to dominate this as far
as may be.   We are all for progress, but we each define it in his
own way.   Hence one man of industrial energy builds more factories
or slums, another as naturally more breweries to supply them; and
in municipal or national council his line of action, conscious or
unconscious, remains congruent with these.   Representative government fails to yield all that its inventors hoped of it, simply
because it is so tolerably representative of its majorities; and there
is thus great truth in the common consolation that our municipal
governments, like larger ones, are seldom much worse than we
deserve.   Each social formation, through each of its material
activities, exerts its influence upon the civic whole; and each of its
ideas and ideals wins also its place and power.   At one time the

legal and punitive point of view, directing itself mainly to individual cases, or the philanthropic, palliating sufferings, dispute the foremost places; and now in their turn hygienic or educational endeavours arise, towards treating causes instead of waiting for consequences.   Such endeavours are still undeniably too vague in thought, too crude in practice, and the enthusiast of hygiene or education or temperance may have much to answer for.   But so, also, has he who stands outside of the actual civic field, whether as philistine or aesthete, utopist or cynic, party politician or "mugwump."   Between all these extremes it is for the united forces of civic survey and civic service to find the middle course.

|114| We observe then in the actual city, as among its future citizens, that our action is generally the attempt to mould both alike to some past or passing social formation, and, therefore, usually towards the type to which our interest and our survey incline, be this in our own city or more probably in some earlier one.   Even in the actual passing detail of party politics we are often reminded how directly continuous are the rivals with puritan London, with royalist Oxford; but still more is this the case throughout the history of thought and action, and the intenser the more plainly; for it is in his highest moments of conviction and decision that the Puritan feels most in sympathy with the law or the prophets of Jerusalem, the scholar with Athens; or that the man of action—be he the first French republican or the latest imperialist—most frankly draws his inspiration from the corresponding developments of Paris.   It is a commonplace of psychology that our thought is and must be anthropomorphic; a commonplace of history that it has been Hebraomorphic, Hellenomorphic, Latinomorphic, and so on by turns.

This view has often been well worked out by the historian of inventions and discoveries, of customs or laws, of policies or religions, as by the historian of language or the fine arts.   What we still commonly need, however, is to carry this view clearly into our own city and its institutions, its streets and schools and homes, until either in the private spending or public voting of the smallest sum we know exactly whether we are so far determining expenditure and influence towards enlarging, say, the influence and example of renascent Florence in one generation or of decadent Versailles in another.   There is no danger of awaking this consciousness too fully; for since we have ceased consciously to cite and utilise the high examples of history we have been the more faithfully, because sub-consciously and automatically, continuing and extending later and lower developments.

E–CITIES, PRESENT AND FUTURE

Hence, after a Liberal and an Imperial generation, each happy in their respective visions of wealth and expanding great- |115| ness, the current renewal of civic interests naturally takes the form of an awakening survey of our actual environment.   First, a literal mapping of its regional elements, and then an historic interpretation of these—not, alas, merely or mainly in terms of the cities of sacred or classic tradition, nor of the Mediaeval or Renaissance cities which followed these, but as stupendous extensions of the mediaeval Ghetto, of the Wapping Stairs, of the Lancashire factories and of the Black Country, relieved by the coarse jollities of Restoration London, and adorned for the most part, with debased survivals from the Italian and the French Renaissance.   There is thus no more question in our civic discussions of "bringing in" or "leaving out" geography or history; we have been too long unconscious of them, as was M. Jourdain of his speaking in prose.

But what of the opening Future? May its coming social developments not be discerned by the careful observer in germs and buds already formed or forming, or deduced by the thinker from sociological principles?   I believe in large measure both; yet cannot within these limits attempt to justify either.   Enough for the present, if it be admitted that the practical man in his thought and action in the present is mainly the as yet too unconscious child of the past, and that in the city he is still working within the grasp of natural conditions.

To realise the geographic and historic factors of our city's life is thus the first step to comprehension of the present, one indispensable to any attempt at the scientific forecast of the future, which must avoid as far as it can the dangers of mere utopianism.

F–LITERATURE OF CIVICS

No discussion of the preliminaries and fundamentals of Civics can omit some consideration of the vast and ever growing literature of

cities.   But how are we to utilise this?   How continue it?   How
co-ordinate it with the needed independent and first-hand survey
of city by city?   And how apply this whole knowledge of past and
present towards civic action?

The answer must plainly be a concrete one.   Every city |116|
however small, has already a copious literature of its topography
and history in the past; one, in fact, so ample that its mere
bibliography may readily fill a goodly volume,* to which the
specialist will long be adding fresh entries. This mass of literature
may next be viewed as the material for a comprehensive monograph,
well enriched with maps and illustrations, such as many cities can
boast; and this again may be condensed into a guide-book.   Guide-
books have long been excellent in their descriptive and historical
detail, and are becoming increasingly interpretative also, especially
since Mr. Grant Allen transferred his evolutionary insight and his
expository clearness from natural to civic history.

After this general and preliminary survey of geographic environment and historic development, there nowadays begins to appear
the material of a complementary and contemporary volume, the
Social Survey proper.   Towards this, statistical materials are partly
to be found amid parliamentary and municipal reports and returns,
economic journals and the like, but a fresh and first-hand survey
in detail is obviously necessary.   In this class of literature, Mr.
Booth's monumental Survey of London, followed by others, such as
Mr. Rowntree's of York, have already been so widely stimulating
and suggestive that it may safely be predicted that before many
years the Social Survey of any given city will be as easily and
naturally obtainable as is at present its guide-book; and the rationalised census of the present condition of its people, their occupation
and real wages, their family budget and culture-level, should be as
readily ascertainable from the one, as their antecedents understood
or their monuments visited by help of the other.

But these two volumes—"The City: Past and Present,"—are not
enough.   Is not a third volume imaginable and possible, that of the
opening Civic Future?   Having taken full note of places as they
were and are, of things as they have come about, and of people as
they are—of their occupations, families, and institutions, their ideas

*e.g., Erskine Beveridge, LL.D., Bibliography of Dunfermline.—*Dunfermline*,
1902.   8vo.

and ideals—may we not to some extent discern, then patiently plan
out, at length boldly suggest, something of |117| their actual or
potential development?   And may not, must not, such discernment,
such planning, while primarily, of course, for the immediate future,
also take account of the remoter and higher issues which a city's
indefinitely long life and correspondingly needed foresight and
statesmanship involve?   Such a volume would thus differ widely
from the traditional and contemporary "literature of Utopias" in
being regional instead of non-regional, indeed ir-regional and so
realisable, instead of being unrealisable and unattainable altogether.   The theme of such a volume would thus be to indicate the
practicable alternatives, and to select and to define from these the
lines of development of the legitimate *Eu-topia* possible in the given
city, and characteristic of it; obviously, therefore, a very different
thing from a vague *Ou-topia*, concretely realisable nowhere.   Such
abstract counsels of perfection as the descriptions of the ideal city,
from Augustine through More or Campanella and Bacon to Morris,
have been consolatory to many, to others inspiring.   Still, a Utopia
is one thing, a plan for our city improvement is another.

Some concrete, if still fragmentary, materials towards such a
volume are, of course, to be found in all municipal offices, though
scattered between the offices of the city engineer and health officer,
the architect and park superintendent; while the private architect
and landscape gardener, the artist, sometimes even the municipal
voters and their representatives, may all have ideas of their own.
But though our cities are still as a whole planless, their growth as
yet little better than a mere casual accretion and agglomeration, if
not a spreading blight, American and German cities are now increasingly affording examples of comprehensive design of extension and
of internal improvement.   As a specific example of such an attempt
towards the improvement of a British city, one not indeed compre-
hending all aspects of its life, but detailed and reasoned so far as
it goes, and expressing that continuity of past and present into
future which has been above argued for, I am permitted by the
courtesy of the Carnegie Dunfermline Trust to lay on the Society's
library table an early copy of a recent study of practicable possibilities in a city typically suitable for consideration from the present
standpoint, since presenting within a moderate and readily intelli-
gible |118| scale a very marked combination of historic interests,

and of contemporary and growing activity, both industrial and cultural, with hopeful civic outlook.

That co-adjustment of social survey and social service which has been above argued for as the essential idea of civics as applied sociology is thus no abstract principle, but a concrete and practicable method.   Yet it is one not lacking in generality of application. For what we have reached is really the conception of an *Encyclopaedia Civica*, to which each city should contribute the Trilogy of its Past, its Present, and its Future.   Better far, as life transcends books, we may see, and yet more, forsee, the growth of civic consciousness and conscience, the awakening of citizenship towards civic renascence.   All this the production of such volumes would at one imply and inspire—life ever producing its appropriate expression in literature, and literature reacting upon the ennoblement of life.

Apart altogether from what may be the quality and defects of particular volumes, such as those cited as examples of each part of such a proposed civic trilogy, one as yet nowhere complete, the very conception of such a possible threefold series may be of some service.   For this would present a continuous whole, at once sociological and civic—the views and the resources of the scholar and the educationist with their treasures of historic culture, of the man of action with his mastery of immediate affairs, of the thinker with his vision of the opening future, now all co-ordinated by help of the design of the artist, and thence to be gradually realised in the growing heritage of the city, the enlarging life of the citizen.

NOTE.—As an example of the concrete application to a particular city, of the sociological methods and principles indicated in the above paper, Prof. Geddes exhibited an illustrated volume embodying the results of his studies and designs towards the improvement of Dunfermline, under the Trust recently established by Mr. Carnegie.   This has since been published:

P. GEDDES.   City Development.   Park Gardens and Culture Institutes; a Report to the Carnegie Dunfermline Trust.   With 138 illustrations.   Edinburgh, etc.. 1904.

The Chairman (MR. CHARLES BOOTH) in opening the discussion said:

The paper we have just heard read is one of the most complete and charming papers on a great and interesting subject I have ever heard.   I think you will all agree in this, and I hope the discussion which follows will emphasise and, if that is possible, add to the wealth of ideas that this paper contains.

MR EBENEZER HOWARD

(Founder of the Garden City Association) said:

I have read and re-read—in the proof forwarded to me—Professor Geddes' wonderfully luminous and picturesque paper with much interest.   He has given us a graphic description of the geographic process which leads to the development of the city.   We see vividly the gradual stages by which the city grows and swells, with the descent of the population from the hillsides into the valleys, even as the river which flows through the city is fed continually by the streams which flow down to it.   But is there not this essential difference between the gathering waters of heaven, as they pour into the great city, and the gathering tide of population, which follows the path of the waters?   The waters flow through the city on, on toward the mighty ocean, and are then gradually gathered upward into the soft embraces of the clouds and wafted back again to the hills, whence they flow down once more to the valleys.   But the living stream of men, women, and children flows from the country-side and leaves it more and more bare of active, vigorous, healthy life: it does not, like the waters, "return again to cover the earth," but moves ever on to the great city, and from thence, at least for the great majority, there is no chance of more than, at best, a very short stay in the country.   No: the tide flows resistlessly

91

|120| onward to make more crowded our overcrowded tenements, to enlarge our overgrown cities, to cause suburb to spread beyond suburb, to submerge more and more the beautiful fields and hilly slopes which used to lie near the busy life of the people, to make the atmosphere more foul, and the task of the social reformer more and yet more difficult.

But surely there must be a way, could we but discover it, of imitating the skill and bountifulness of Nature, by creating channels through which some of our population shall be attracted back to the fields; so that there shall be a stream of population pouring from the city into the country, till a healthy balance is restored, and we have solved the twin problems of rural depopulation and of the overcrowded, overgrown city.

This brings me to the second branch of Prof. Geddes' paper, the historical.   The Professor reminds us how vestiges of one civilisation lie super-imposed upon another, like geological strata, and asks.   "Understanding the present as the development of the past, are we not preparing also to understand the future as the development of the present?"   Following this line of thought, I venture to suggest that while the age in which we live is the age of the great, closely-compacted, overcrowded city, there are already signs, for those who can read them, of a coming change so great and so momentous that the twentieth century will be known as the period of the great exodus, the return to the land, the period when by a great and conscious effort a new fabric of civilisation shall be reared by those who knew how to apply the knowledge gained by "Social Survey to Social Service."   What are the signs?   What words can we place under the head of "Incipient" in Prof. Geddes' diagram? I would suggest, for one of Prof. Geddes' interrogation marks might be substituted "Decentralisation of Industry"—as a great, but yet incipient movement, represented by Port Sunlight, Bournville, Garden City.   For there are now many agencies at work making for industrial decentralisation.   Industries are being driven out of the great towns by the excessive rents and rates which have to be paid there—by the difficulty of obtaining adequate space for the modern factory, a one-storey building; and for the homes of our workers, which must be vastly different to what they now are if England is to maintain her place among the nations.   And while factories are being driven from the city, they are also being attracted to the country by its newly-discovered potentialities. Thus Messrs. Lever Brothers, crowded out of Warrington, established an entirely new town on a new site at Port Sunlight; and, because the site was new and raw, it was therefore possible for Mr. Lever to plan his little town with a single eye to the best and most desirable conditions, alike from an industrial and a health and housing point of view. And the same is true of Bournville. Bournville is one of the most beautiful villages in the world, largely again because of the potentialities of a new site acquired for the definite purpose of building thereon a village in which overcrowding shall be deliberately and permanently prevented, |121| and in which work inside the factory may be varied by work in the garden. Now that these successful experiments have been carried out in this country, is it not time that the idea of establishing new industries on new sites, and of surrounding those industries with healthy homes, should be carried forward on a larger scale, with wider and more concerted aims—carried forward, too, in such a manner as to make it possible for the small manufacturer to take part in a movement which has proved to be so beneficial alike to employer and employed? It is out of this thought that the Garden City idea has grown, an idea now in course of being fulfilled. Three thousand eight hundred acres of land, or nearly ten times the area of Bournville or Port Sunlight, have been acquired in Hertfordshire, two miles west of the town of Hitchin, and on the branch line of railway between that town and Cambridge. State aid has not been sought; that would indeed be weary work. But a company has been formed, through the untiring efforts of the Garden City Association; plans for the town have been carefully prepared, plans which, of course, have regard to the contours of the land (which were first taken, showing every change of level of five feet), to the preservation of its natural beauties—its trees and the picturesque villages of Norton and Willian; to the necessity for railway sidings and railway station, now, thanks to the Great Northern Railway, already provided; to the making of roads of easy gradient and of suitable width, affording access to different parts of the estate, actual work on which is progressing; the careful guarding from contamination of our water supply, already proved to be abundant; the provision of a reservoir of suitable elevation, now in course of construction; a system of drainage, about to be started with; the provision of parks and playgrounds within the town, as well as a wide belt of agricultural land around it; sites for homes for 30,000 persons, with good sized gardens.   About six cottages have already been built, not by the Company but by private enterprise, while many others are just about to be started upon; the setting apart of sites for schools, churches, and other public buildings, while plans are in preparation for lighting the town, as well as for providing it with motive power.

The programme which I have sketched out is certainly not too bold or comprehensive for the British race.   If a hundredth part of the organising skill which the Japanese and the Russians are showing in the great war now in progress were shown by ourselves as citizens in our great civil war against disease and dirt, poverty and overcrowding, we could not only build many new cities on the best models, but could also bring our old towns into line with the new and better order.   Prof. Geddes wishes well, I know, to the Garden City Association, a propagandist body, and to its first child, the Garden City Company; and I am sure you will all unite with me in the hope that the best and most lasting success may crown the generous gift of Mr. Carnegie of £500,000 to the City of Dunfermline, and reward the efforts of the Trustees and of Prof. Geddes to make, by the application of modern |122| skill, science and art, the ancient city of Dunfermline a centre of sweetness and light, stimulating us all to higher and yet higher efforts to secure civic, national and imperial well-being.

MR. C. H. GRINLING said:

Like most of the audience, doubtless, he came not to speak but to draw ever fresh inspiration from Prof. Geddes.   But there was one aspect of the subject he would like to bring out and emphasise. He referred to the sociological institute, which, under the name of the Outlook Tower, had grown up in connection with the School of Sociology which Prof. Geddes had founded and developed in Edinburgh.   That institute was at once an organisation for teaching and for research, for social education, and for civic action.   It was, in fact, a concrete and working application of the principle indicated in the paper as the very foundation of Civics—"social survey for social service."   And, seeing that the Outlook Tower was an institution designed in every respect for application to any given locality, he urged the Sociological Society to advocate its general extension, so that no region should be without its own sociological institute or Outlook Tower.

If one individual could accomplish so much, what could not be accomplished by the sociologists of our day who would concentrate themselves, each on his own locality, not necessarily to do the work, but to give the inspiration which would call out the work of collecting just that material which Prof. Geddes suggested all through his paper was one of the great needs of our time?   And so one hoped that papers of this kind would not merely lead to discussion, but to workers accumulating results of this kind, giving the inspiration to others, and thus laying up treasures for the sociologists of the future for their interpretation.   Thus, the Sociological Society should be not only the one scientific society in constant touch with all the leading brains over the country, but it should be an inspiration, as Prof. Geddes has himself been, to groups of workers everywhere for just the kind of work which the Sociological Society has been founded to develop.

MR. J. M. ROBERTSON said:

I would first add my tribute to this extremely interesting and stimulating paper.   It recalled confabulations I had with Prof. Geddes, many years ago, when he was first formulating in Edinburgh those ideas which have since become so widely known.   I would like, however, to suggest a few criticisms.   The paper is, broadly speaking, an application of the view of a biologist to Sociology. It is not so much an application of Darwin's view as that of Von Baer.   Prof. Geddes has characterised his paper as one of elementary preliminaries, but he has really contributed a paper that |123| would form part of a preliminary study in a series of studies in Sociology. The paper does not quite bear out its title: "Civics: as Applied Sociology."   The application has not begun.   The somewhat disparaging remarks on encyclopaedias of general knowledge, further, might well be applied to the scheme of an encyclopaedia of the natural history of every city and every village as an original centre.   This atomism will not help Sociology.   Had he to master all that, the sociologist's life would be a burden not to be borne, and we would never get to applied sociology at all.   There is a danger, too, in following this line, of fastening attention on one stage of evolution and leaving it there.   The true principle is that evolution is eternal and continuous; and I think harm may be done, possibly, when you take, say, the phenomenon of the communication of general knowledge in schools and call it a derivation from the French *Encyclopedie.* Why leave it there? Where did that come from? If you are going to trace the simple evolution of civic forms, if you are to trace how they have come about, it will not do to stick at a given point. This is a survival of that. That is a survival of something else. The French *Encyclopedie* will have to be traced back to the encyclopædia of the mediæval period; and even to the still earlier period of Isidore of Seville. Then again, there is a danger, I think, analogous to the danger met with in early botany—the danger of confusing a resemblance with a relationship. It is extremely interesting to speculate that the Place de l'Etoile is an evolution from the plan of the game-forest, with its shooting avenues radiating from a centre, but it would be difficult to show that there is any historical connection. The thing is not proved.

Of course, the vital question is not this tracing of evolution. The question is: Is "Civics" to be only the study of forms? If so, Sociology is a dead science, and will effect little practical good until it is vivified by such suggestions as Mr. Crane has put in his paper. Mr. Walter Crane brought in a vital question when he said: "How are you going to modify the values of your civic life unless you grapple with political problems?" I am not forgetting that Prof. Geddes promises to deal in another paper with the civics of the future; but I insist that it will have to grapple with political questions. As he says, a city is not a place, but "a drama in time." The question for the sociological student of history is: How has this inequality of wealth and of service arisen, and how is it to be prevented in the future? That is the problem we have to study if we wish to make sociology a vital interest. A definition of progress is really the first step in sociology. Prof. Geddes' next paper should give us a definition of progress, and it is better that we begin to fight over a definition of progress, in order to get a dynamic agreement, than that we should multiply the archæological study of many towns. I admit that it is very interesting. In travelling in South Africa, I often tried to gather how communities began; what, for example, was the nucleus of this or that village. It was surprising how very few had an idea of any nucleus at all.

I deprecate the idea, however, that |124| we are all to amass an enormous accumulation of such researches.   Mr. Booth's single compilation for London is a study for years; but Mr. Booth's admirable investigation of the difficulties of life among the poor of London does not of itself give any new impulse to the solution of the problem of London.   It merely gives exact knowledge in place of general knowledge.   The problem of sociology arose on the general knowledge.   I fear lest the work of sociology should run to an extension of this admirable study instead of to the stimulation of action taken on that particular knowledge, or on more general knowledge.   We all knew there was plenty of poverty, and how it was caused.   We all had ideals as to how it was to be got rid of in the future; but the question is: Is the collection of detail or the prescription of social method the kind of activity that the Sociological Society is to take up?

SIR THOMAS BARCLAY said:
I am not sure that I agree with Mr. Robertson that it is desirable to define either "progress" or "civilisation."   On the whole, their chances lie rather in the great variety of ideas of what constitutes them than in any hard-and-fast notion of their meaning.   They are generalisations of what is, rather than an object towards which effort should tend.   But neither do I agree with Prof. Geddes' restriction of "civics" to the mere outward part of municipal effort.   In America the word "civics" is applied to the rights and duties of citizens, and I should like to see Prof. Geddes include in Civics the connection between citizen life and the outward improvement of cities.   I am sure, however, Professor Geddes, as a practical man, will deal rather with realities than theoretical views on the subject for which he has done so much himself.   Edinburgh owes more than many are willing to admit to Prof. Geddes.   I think Ramsay Lodge one of the greatest embellishments of the Castle Hill in Edinburgh.   I hope he will now be successful in doing something still more admirable for my native town of Dunfermline.   My friend Mr. Carnegie, whose native town it also is, I believe intends to show by an object lesson what can be done for all cities.   Prof. Geddes is helping him in this work with his suggestions.   I hope they will be carried out.   In America there are several very beautiful cities. No one can ever forget Washington, which is truly a garden city.

No money is spared in America to beautify and healthify (excuse the barbarism) the habitations of the thousands. A beautiful city is an investment for health, intellect, imagination. Genius all the world over is associated, wherever it has been connected with cities, with beautiful cities. To grow up among things of beauty ennobles the population. But I should like to see Prof. Geddes extend his projects for Dunfermline to the population itself. Most of you know what Mr. Henderson did to utilise the Edinburgh |125| police in the care of children. The future of the country depends upon them. The subject is too serious to continue to be left to the haphazard mercies of indifferent parents. Every child born is an agent for good or for evil among the community, and the community cannot afford to neglect how it is brought up, the circumstances in which it has its being, the environment from which it derives its character and tendencies. Necessity may be the mother of invention, but need of food and insufficient clothing develop in the child an inventiveness that is not for the good of the community. It seems a matter of too great an importance to be left even to private initiative, as was done under Mr. Henderson's régime in Edinburgh; but everywhere else, or nearly so, very little is done by even private initiative for the protection of the children against their vicious environment. In short, I do not think that civics, in the sense in which my friend Prof. Geddes treats it, is a complete subject at all. Civics, to my mind, includes everything that relates to the citizen. Everywhere something is being done in one direction or another to make them capable, prosperous, and happy. In America happiness is taught in the schools. Every schoolmaster's and schoolmistress's first duty is to set an example of a happy frame of mind; smiling and laughing are encouraged, and it is not thought that the glum face is at all necessary for the serious business of life. In fact, the glum face is a disqualification; is associated with failure, and bad luck and ill-nature. In Germany the schoolmaster is in the first place a trainer of the body. One of his chief duties is to watch and prevent the deterioration of the eyesight, to promote the development of the lungs, to prevent spinal deviation. The second part of his business is to watch over the character of the child, and only the third part is to ram knowledge into the poor little mind. And wherever you go over the world you will find something in the course of being done in civics, as I understand the subject.   I thank Prof. Geddes for what he is doing for Dunfermline, and hope he will understand "progress" without requiring to define it.

DR. J. LIONEL TAYLER

(Author of "*Aspects of Social Evolution*") said:

While agreeing with Prof. Geddes in his belief in the importance of institutional and geographical studies as a basis for the investigation of the development of cities, it yet seems to me that these studies cannot prove of supreme value to society unless they are accompanied by a detailed examination of the *natural* characteristics of all individuals who have been born into and existed in, or merely dwelt in, these surroundings.   It is not enough to trace out, however accurately, the various stages of a town's growth from its commencement to the present time, because *the cause* of |126| the evolution of any city aggregate lies deeper, is in large part animate, and not inanimate, in character.   The value of the surroundings depends at least as much upon the capacity of the individual citizen, singly and collectively, to utilise what he or she is brought in contact with as upon the peculiarities of these surroundings themselves.   Place, tradition, social organisation, individual development, education, are factors in town evolution that cannot safely be overlooked, and they all vary from age to age and in place and place.

If it were possible to completely exchange the inhabitants of a large town in England with those of an equally large town in France two groups of changes would become more or less rapidly observable: (1) the French and English citizens would adapt themselves, as far as they desired and were able, to their altered conditions; (2) the characteristics of both towns would gradually change, in spite of geographical position, in response to the altered human needs. Similarly, a town composed of individuals who are naturally uncultured and unprogressive will tend to preserve its uncultured and unprogressive characters more than another that has alert citizens to carry on its activities.   Every profession and every trade tends to foster its own social atmosphere; and towns will vary with their industrial life, and individuals favourably disposed to this atmosphere will come to the town, and those unfavourably inclined to it will leave.   *These changing citizens, as they act upon and react*

to their surroundings and vary in their powers age by age, are
the real evolvers of the conditions in which they dwell; hence the
citizen must not be omitted from our study if we are to understand
city growth.

In other words, I think that every investigation of civic, and for
that matter country life should be studied from two aspects: (1) to
note the peculiarities, growth and development of the material, non-
living and non-thinking elements in the problem—the buildings,
their geographical position, their age, their fitness for past and
present life, and the distinctive local features that are evolving or
retrogressing with the multiplication of some trades and industries
and the decline of others in each area that is studied; (2) the change
in the quality of the citizens themselves through racial, educational,
and other factors, noting how far ideals are altering, not only in the
mass of individuals taken as a whole, but also by examining the
changing outlook in every trade and profession.   With these two
parallel lines of investigation to study, we could then determine how
far environment—social and climatic—how far racial and individual
characteristics have been powerful in the moulding of the fabric
around us.

With these two lines of study to our hands, we could predict the
vitality, the growing power, and the future possibilities of the social
life of which we are a tiny though not an insignificant part; we
could, knowing something of the response that we make to that
which surrounds us, form some estimate of how the future ages will
develop, and, knowing the |127| intensity of the different national
desires for progress *and the causes which are likely to arouse such
desires*, we could realise what will stimulate and what will retard
all that is best in our civic life.

PROFESSOR EARL BARNES (in moving a vote of thanks) said:
For years I have been accumulating a debt of obligation to Prof.
Geddes for ideas, suggestions, and large synthesis of life, and it gives
me special pleasure to voice the feeling of this meeting concerning
the paper read to us this afternoon.   To me, as an American, it is
especially interesting to hear this presentation of life as an organic
whole.   Life is but a period of education, and if there is nothing
behind this present moment of life it is all extremely insignificant.
To an American, who has lived at No. 1067 in 63rd Street, Phila-

delphia, and at No. 1718 in G Street, in Washington, it is profoundly interesting to think of the possibility of a man's so living that his whole existence shall be significant, so that the realities of his world, geographical, geological, and material, and all that long development of humanity through the historic past—that all these things will be really and truly significant to him. Prof. Geddes has himself shown us that is possible. Any man who has gone to Edinburgh and seen the restoration of the old life that has been carried out there under his hand knows it can be done. I suppose we all came here to hear Professor Geddes speak on practical affairs because his name is now connected with the plans for making a city that shall be really expressive of all its potentialities to all of its people. I am personally profoundly grateful to him for his paper; and I move you that he be given a very hearty vote of thanks.

The Chairman. (MR. CHARLES BOOTH), in closing the discussion, said: I myself entirely agree with what Mr Robertson has said as to the extreme difficulty of bringing investigations of the kind referred to, to practical conclusions—practical points. Practical work at present needs the most attention. I perhaps am too old to do it, but I feel the attraction of that kind of work, and that was one reason I was sorry Mr Loch had to leave before we could hear what he might have to say. The description I have given of London does seem to be a foggy labyrinth I agree, but nevertheless I cannot but think that we do require a complete conception if we are to do the definite work of putting different people in their proper places in an organic whole, such as a city is. I do not think we can do without it, and I regard the paper of this evening as an important con- |128| tribution to that complete conception which I feel we need. I should like each worker and thinker to have and to know his place in the scheme of civic improvement; and I think it perfectly possible for every man to know what it is that he is trying to do, what contribution it is that he ought to give to that joint life which is called here civics, which is the life of a city and the life in the city. One man cannot possibly concentrate it all in himself. Within a society such as the Sociological Society a general scheme is possible in which each individual and each society shall play its acknowledged and recognised part. It does not follow that the work done in one city can apply as an example to another. Indi-

viduality has too strong a hold; but each town may work out
something for itself.   I have been very much interested in the work
which Mr. Rowntree has done in York, on which he was kind enough
to consult me.   He entered upon it on quite other grounds from
mine, but so far as the ground was common between him and me
we tried to have a common basis.   Those of you who have not read
Mr. Horsfall's volumes on Manchester would do well to do so.
Prof. Geddes gave us a vivid picture of a larger regional unit which
culminates geographically in the city as industrial climax.   In his
particular instance he referred, I take, to Dundee.   In Dundee there
is at this moment an inquiry being started, and I am in commu-
nication with those who are doing it, and I hope it will add
something to the completeness of the picture we have of that city.
In Dundee they have excessive difficulties in respect to crowding
and female labour.   What I suggested was, that they should make
a special study of such circumstances as are special to Dundee.
Labour there is very largely sack-making and jute manufacture, and
there is a great deal of girl labour; and that is one of the special
subjects that will be considered in that inquiry.

Then, with regard to the preservation of such of the natural
beauties that do remain even quite near to busy town centres, surely
it is of the greatest importance that they should be watched and
protected and preserved.   Prof. Geddes has contributed a portion
of his practical work to that practical question at Dunfermline.
His charming volume on Dunfermline ("A Study in City Development") shows what beautiful features there are near Dunfermline,
and how much may be done to preserve and improve them in ways
that are most interesting to study.   His use of photography in this
matter is extraordinarily successful.   Prof. Geddes has photo-
graphed a scene as it now is, with its background and distance and
its squalid foreground, already ruined by the debris of the city—old
tin pots and every |129| kind of rubbish—thrown down by the side
of the stream, which is naturally beautiful.   By manipulating the
photographic plates he wipes out that which he does not want and
introduces other features, including a little waterfall; and you have,
instead of a miserable suburb, a dignified park.   Well now, that is
practical work.   It has in it that element which he has described
by a question-mark in his diagram, the element of forecast.   You
have the same idea in Manchester, in Mr. Horsfall's work.   They

have laid out their map of Manchester and shown in what way it may develop, so as not to spoil the beauty that remains on two sides of Manchester.   There is really exquisitely beautiful natural scenery close to Manchester, which may be entirely spoiled or preserved, according as a forecast is made and forethought taken. This is not a question on which there is reason to think that people will disagree.   The difficulties are always supposed to be financial. It is a sad thing that we should be so hampered by our methods of finance that we throw away opportunities to retain these actual beauties which undoubtedly add to the actual money value of a district.   I cannot suppose that the way in which cities are laid out with narrow streets really results in an increase of value.   The surroundings of our cities are undeveloped estates, which we have only to agree amongst ourselves how to lay out, and everybody would benefit by such joint action.   There is an excellent illustration in regard to that in Mr. Horsfall's work in connection with Germany.   It must be said that from Germany there is a great deal to learn in civic matters.   In one of its towns the properties lie in extraordinarily long strips   It is the final result of properties having been measured by the length of the plough's run.   When that method is applied to town sites, it is not convenient for streets; and there are some quarters in this German town ruined in this way, and the people have agreed together to improve matters. Every owner is to be given credit for his share in the total value of the improvement that is found to accrue from the re-arrangement of these undesirable divisions, and any difference of opinion as to the just share and proportion is to be referred to an impartial arbitrator.   All the owners will gain, though some a little more than others.   That is an example that we may do well to try and follow, and in some way or other improve the money value, and social value, and hygienic value of towns, and if necessary compel the carrying out of improvements when some few might be disposed to hold out against them.

From PROF. BALDWIN BROWN
(Professor of Fine Art in the University of Edinburgh)

I am glad of this opportunity of saying how cordially I agree with the method adopted by my friend Professor Geddes in dealing with the life of cities. He treats the modern community and its material shell as things of organic growth, with a past and a future as well as a present, whereas we too often see these wider considerations ignored in favour of some exigency of the moment. A historic British town has recently furnished a striking object-lesson in this connection. The town possesses portions of an ancient city wall and fosse that were made at a time when the town was, for the moment, the most important in Great Britain. Yet the Town Council, a year ago, destroyed part of this wall and filled a section of the fosse for the purpose of providing a site for a new elementary school. No doubt, in that school, books "approved by the Department" will instruct scholars in the past history of the burgh, but the living witness of that history must first of all be carefully obliterated. All the rest of this ancient and historic enceinte was condemned a few weeks ago to complete destruction, merely on the plea that the site would be convenient for workmen's dwellings. The monument has now been saved, but it has taken the whole country to do it!

Here were chosen officials, governors of no mean city, absolutely oblivious of these important interests committed to their care, and all for want of having drilled into them these broader views which Professor Geddes puts forward so well.

He has himself done practical work in Edinburgh on the lines he lays down, and I have lately had occasion to note, and call attention to the advantage to the city of much wise conservatism in regard to our older buildings which he and his associates have shown.

In Edinburgh we have the advantage that our older monuments, |131| in which so much of the past life of the city is enshrined, are firm and solid; and it takes some trouble to knock them down. Hence for some time to come we shall preserve here object-lessons in civic development that will be of interest to the country at large.

From MR. WALTER CRANE
(President of Arts and Crafts Exhibition Society)

Professor Geddes' very interesting "Study in City Development" is highly suggestive, and shows how great a difference thoughtful and tasteful treatment might make in dealing with such problems.   It is sad to think of the opportunities wasted, and of the more ignorant and often too hasty clearances for traffic which have often been apparently the sole motives in city improvement.   The conservation of historic buildings, whenever possible, the planting of trees along our streets, the laying out of gardens, the insistence upon a proportional amount of air and open space to new buildings would go a long way towards making our bricks-and-mortar joyless wildernesses into something human and habitable.

Whether, under favourable circumstances and the rare public spirit of private owners, much can be done, or to any wide extent, so long as absolute individual ownership in land and ground values is allowed, seems to me very doubtful.   We cannot hope to see great social improvements without great economic changes, but every effort in the direction of improving the beauty of our cities is welcome to all who have the well-being of the community at heart; and such work as Prof. Geddes is doing should arouse the keenest interest and the earnest attention of all who realise its immense social importance.

From MR. J. H. HARLEY, M.A.

If sociology is ever to vindicate itself as an art, it must be able to analyse and explain the present, and to some extent at least to cast the horoscope of the future.   It must feel its way through all the tangled labyrinths of city life, and show us where we have arrived and whither we are going.   But this is exactly the part of Professor Geddes' Applied Sociology where he becomes most vague and unsatisfactory.   'Enough for the present," we are told, "if it be admitted that the practical man in his thought and action in the present is mainly as yet the too unconscious child of the past, and that in the city he is still working within the grasp of natural conditions." Now we must all be willing to admit that the present is the child of the past, and that we cannot adequately understand |132| the present until we have led up to the present by the study of its antecedents more and less remote.   But what Professor Geddes fails to bring out is that it is only in the present or the more immediate past that the City has really become a City in the modern sense of the word.   The City as City is a product of the Industrial Revolution.   Its huge and casual assemblages of human life, its overcrowding, its poverty line, its East End and its West End, its infantile mortality, its trades massed in their own particular districts, it aliens, its criminals and its vices—all these problems of social pathology arise from the fact that the conditions of modern industry have brought people together who have few interests in common, and who were compelled to arrange themselves in some kind of decent order within a limited area, without sufficient time being given to evolve a suitable environment, or to prepare themselves for the environment which they actually found on every side of them.   London in the past, therefore, cannot help us so very much to solve the riddles of London in the present, because London in the past had not developed these social growths or offered a mature ground to those social parasites which make us sometimes despair of being able to get much insight into the London of the present.

The fact seems to be that Prof. Geddes conceives sociology too much as a primary and too little as a secondary science.   He defines applied sociology as the application of social survey to social science, when social ratiocination or social philosophy are needed before one can be said to have gauged the extent of the influence which this comprehensive science may have in our actual practice or on our Budget of the future.   No doubt, "observation, so far from excluding interpretation, is just the very means of preparing for it," but this preparation must be made in the various specialisms which make up the complete or encyclopaedic science of sociology.   To me it seems an unwarrantable narrowing of the scope or significance of sociology to say that there is no better method available of teaching it "than that of regional survey, historical as well as geographical." Surely "regional survey" is the appropriate method in the very simplest and most concrete parts of the complete science of sociology, and even when we come to history proper we must do very much more than make a regional survey. It is very interesting, no doubt, to "survey" history in the course of a summer ramble to the ruins of some old monastery, but unless the monks had kept records of what had been done there in bygone days, the mere outward survey will not carry us further than Prof. Geddes is carried in the very general map which he makes of the whole field of history. In other words, history, in any proper sense, demands more than "survey" in Prof. Geddes' sense of the word. It calls to its aid linguistics, criticism, archaeology, jurisprudence, and politics—there must be comparison and criticism as well as "survey." History is the laboratory in which the sociologist sees his social experiments working out their |133| results, and history is to the sociologist what experiment is to the physician, or the comparative method to the biologist.

This being so, the scope of "civics" as "applied sociology" is immensely widened. The present is the child of the past, but we see that it is only in the present that such ancient groups as the colony of Hanseatic merchants in Old London have shown us what has been the ultimate significance of their embryological life. The modern city bristles with sociological problems which demand a knowledge of most of the specialisms included in the complete science of sociology, and almost invite us to cast the horoscope of the future. We see, as Booth and Rowntree saw before us, the poverty line like a fiery portent at every point of our study, and we are led finally to ask ourselves whether M. Arthur Bauer was not right in choosing the title "Les Classes Sociales" as the most characteristic title he could give to his recent and most suggestive analysis of the general characteristics of social life.

From MR. T. C. HORSFALL
(President, Manchester Citizen's Association, &c.)

The teaching of the paper seems to me to be most sound and helpful. The town of the future—I trust of the near future—must by means of its schools, its museums, and galleries, its playgrounds, parks and gymnasia, its baths, its wide tree-planted streets and the belt of unspoilt country which must surround it, bring all its inhabitants in some degree under the *best* influences of all the regions and all the stages of civilisation, the influences of which, but not the best influences, contribute, and have contributed, to make our towns what they are.

From H. OSMAN NEWLAND
(Author of "*A Short History of Citizenship*")

The failures of democratic governments in the past have been attributable, in part, to the lack of intelligence and self-consciousness among the mass of those who were given a voice in the government of their country.   Citizenship, like morality, was allowed to grow by instinct; it was never systematised as a science, or applied as an art.   Sparta and Athens approached towards a system of civics much less elaborate than that expounded by Professor Geddes; but in Sparta citizenship became inseparable from Nationalism, and in Athens it scarcely rose above Municipalism.   In more modern times, civic education has had to encounter the same difficulty as in America, where the young citizen's first duty is to salute his flag, and as in London, where "Civics" is distributed in doles of local |134| history in which the municipality plays a part altogether out of proportion to its relation to the country, the age, and the world.   Civics, as the applied sociology of each individual and each body of interests, has but begun to be dreamed of; and before it can be properly developed it is desirable, if not necessary, that the general public should know something more than at present both of the historic development of the "civic" idea, and of the psychology of aggregations as differentiated from the psychology of the individual.   Not until we can make "the man in the street" a conscious citizen, instead of a political automaton, shall be be able to enlist his sympathies with "Civics"; and without those sympathics the sociologist's "Civics" will, I fear, be but partial and inaccurate.

From MR. G. BISSET SMITH
(H.M. Registration Examiner for East of Scotland).

There is an elusiveness here and there in this paper which has helped to confirm me in the opinion that it is well to emphasise the fact that Prof. Geddes is not only a dreamer of lofty dreams but a doer and a practical initiator.   He has expressed himself not only in words but in art and in architecture, and in educational organisation;

and he has in many ways, sometimes indirectly, influenced scholastic and civic activities.

If from the Outlook Tower he dreams of an idealised Edinburgh he has only to reply to the scoffer who asks, "What have you done?" "*Circumspice!*" There stand the settlements he initiated, the houses beautiful, bright, delectable; and the tower itself is an embodiment of his ideas, an encyclopaedia in stone and in storeys.

We must, in criticising this paper, take into account these attempts towards realisation of its principles. The sociological evolutionist is "concerned primarily with origins, but ultimately and supremely with ideals," we were reminded in a recent paper read before this Society. And in the same paper it was affirmed that, "through the formulation of its larger generalisations as ideals, sociology may hope to achieve the necessary return from theory to practice." Thus, if Civics is applied Sociology, we must rest its claims on these criteria. What, then, we have to ask is:—(1) What actually are the generalisations of the present paper? (2) How far they are warranted by verifiable sociological testimony, and (3) What results do they yield when transformed by the touch of emotion into ideals of action? To attempt an adequate answer to these questions would perhaps transcend the limits of this discussion. But merely to raise these questions of presupposition should tend to clarify the discussion. Coming to detail, I may say, as one whose occupation is demographic, I regret the unavoidable briefness of the reference in "Civics" to a "rationalised census of the present condition of the people."

|135| No one, however, who has studied the concluding portion of "The Evolution of Sex" can accuse Prof. Geddes of ignoring questions of *population*; and his eulogium, written ten years ago, of "Mr. Charles Booth as one of our own latest and best Economists," is familiar to all readers of "Education for Economics and Citizenship." In that extremely suggestive treatise, Prof. Geddes further points out that population must have a primary place in consideration, and that "our studies of the characteristic occupation of region by region are the essential material of a study of its whole civilisation."

Accepting Mr. Branford's definition of *occupation* as "any and every form of human endeavour, past, present, and future," we see that occupation must have a large place in the description, expla-

nation, and forecasting of the evolution of cities—such as Edinburgh, Glasgow, Dundee—in the scheme of survey outlined so
sweepingly in "Civics."

"Life and Labour of the People in London" contains several
general observations almost equally applicable to our largest Scottish
cities, with the demographic conditions of which my official duties
give me special opportunities for becoming familiar and for regional
survey.

In the concluding volume of that great contribution to sociology
Mr. Booth (page 23) remarks:—

"Many influences conspire to cause the poor to multiply almost
in proportion to their poverty, and operate in the other direction
in the case of the better off, almost in proportion to their wealth.
But," says Mr. Booth, "when we bring the death-rate into account
this law no longer holds."

With the poor living under bad conditions in crowded homes the
net increase is diminished.   To those of us who are hopeful of
improvement by eugenics it is pleasing to note that Mr.
Booth—somewhat unlike Mr. Kidd in his well-known "Social
Evolution"—is optimistic in his conclusion that "on the whole it
may fairly be expected that concurrently with a rising standard of
health we may see a fall in birth-rate as well as death-rate, and
thus have no cause to fear, as the result of better sanitation, that
the largest natural increase in population will ever be contributed
by the lowest class."   So the heritage of the city may grow not
only in quantity but also in quality.

From PROFESSOR W. I. THOMAS
(Professor in the University of Chicago, U.S.A.)

From the standpoint of its applicability to new countries like
America, Professor Geddes' programme is inadequate because of its
failure to recognise that a city under these conditions is formed by
a rapid and contemporaneous movement of population, and not by
the lapse of time. |136| The first permanent white settler came to
Chicago precisely one hundred years ago, and the city has a population at present of about two and a quarter millions.   It is here
not a question of slow historic development but of the rapid drifting
towards a certain point, of a population from all quarters of the

globe, and the ethnological standpoint therefore becomes of more importance than the historical.

PROFESSOR GEDDES' reply

I am sincerely glad to be able to express myself in substantial agreement with the majority of my critics, only asking them in turn to recognise that this is but the first half of my subject—an outline of civics as in the first place a matter of science, a geographic and historic survey of past conditions, a corresponding census of present ones—here discussed and insisted on as affording the needful base for their demands upon civics as an art, that of effective social service.

In this respect various critics have in fact anticipated large elements of this future portion of my paper, so that in general views, at least, critics and writer are not so far apart as would appear were the preceding pages submitted as a comprehensive outline of the subject, instead of as its scientific introduction merely.

Of criticisms strictly applicable to this paper as it stands, there are really very few.   I am confident that the chairman must be quite alone in too modestly applying to his great work that description of London itself, with which the paper (Section A, pp. 104-107) opens, since his volumes offer really our first effective clue to the labyrinth, and his method of intensive and specialised regional survey, the intensest searchlight yet brought to bear upon it.

Taking, however, a concrete point of criticism, such as that of the monumental planning of modern Paris as derived from forest rides, the critic need only walk through any French forest, or even to consult a Baedeker, or other guide-book, with its maps of any historic dwelling and its surroundings, from Chantilly or Fontainebleau to minor ones, to see that this plan, originally devised for the pleasure, success and safety |137| of the hunt, and later adapted to domination and defence, became next appreciated as affording the finest possible perspectives of the palatially rebuilt chateau. So that it is not at all a fantastic hypothesis, but an obvious and inevitable conclusion that Napoleon's and Haussman's plans were not at all invented by them for Paris, but were directly imitated from the familiar landscape architecture of the preceding century, which again was but the simplest development from the spacious forest rides of older hunting nobles, laid out without any thought of the architectural and city developments they were destined in later centuries to determine.

The citizen of Washington had till lately often forgotten that the magnificent perspectives of his city are due to the French landscape-architect (Major L'Enfant) whom Washington imported for the express purpose of laying out his capital; yet it is no less clear that this most magnificent of the New World city plans is derived from Old World forest rides, than that its monumental edifices descend from Renaissance and classic exemplars.

I plead indeed for such studies of the plans of any and every city from the point of view of its natural development. The too purely abstract and subjective sociology of the dwellers of great cities like London would in this way be helped by the facts of their own topographic history, already well known and clearly explained by geographer and historian, towards again feeling with the naturalist that even the modern city is but the most complex evolutionary expression and development of the life of Nature.

This view I take to be indeed a commonplace in France; but I account for its apparent unfamiliarity to English readers from the fact of our scanty forests in this island being left practically wild, our nobles not inhabiting them, but the cultivated pasture and arable regions below—planting trees indeed, "plantations," but seldom woods, and practically never forests at all. This again brings out the fact that the French nobles, despite our urban associations with regard to them have belonged far more than ours to the social formation and tradition of the hunter—while ours, despite their love of sports, are yet fundamentally squires, *i.e.*, essentially and historically approximating to the peasants of their villages. The bearing of all this upon their respective history will be obvious. Here again we have the origins of the vivid contrast of the English or so-called naturalistic style of landscape-gardening with the more formal French tradition. Yet in a very true sense we see the former to be even more highly artificial than the latter. |138| The English citizen who may even admit this way of looking at the contrasted city plans of London and Paris may fail, unless he has appreciated the principle here involved, to see why London and Paris houses are so different—the one separate and self-contained, with its door undefended and open upon the street, while the normal Parisian house is a populous, high-piled tenement around a central court, with high *porte cochère* closed by massive oaken doors and guarded by an always vigilant and often surly *concierge*.

A moment of historical reflection suffices to see that the former is the architecture of a long-settled agricultural place, with its spreading undefended villages, in which each household had its separate dwelling, the other a persistence of the Continental fortified city crowded within its walls.

But beyond this we must see the earlier historic, the simpler geographic origins of the French courtyard house as a defensible farmyard, of which the ample space was needed nightly for defence against wild beasts, if not also wilder men, against whom the *concierge* is not only the antique porter but the primitive sentinel.

I may seem unduly to labour such points, yet do so advisedly, in order to emphasise and make clearer the essential thesis of this portion of my paper—that every scientific survey involves a geographic and historic exploration of origins, but that of the still unwritten chapter, that the far-reaching forelook, idealistic yet also critical, which is needful to any true and enduring contribution to social service, is prepared for by habitually imaging the course of evolution in the past.

Speaking personally, as one whose leisure and practical life have alike been largely spent in the study and the preservation of ancient buildings, I may say that this has not been solely, or even essentially, from an antiquarian interest in the historic past, but still more on behalf of a practical interest—that of the idealistic, yet economic, utilitarian, because educational and evolutionary, transformation of our old cities—old Edinburgh, old Dunfermline, and the like—from their present sordid unhygienic failure; and therefore industrial and commercial insufficiency, towards a future equalling if not transcending the recorded greatness of the civic past.

It has, therefore, been to lay the broadest possible basis of evolutionary science, of geographic and historic fact, for what would otherwise be open to ridicule as a Utopian hope, that of Civics as Applied Social Art, that I have insisted at such length above upon Civics as Applied Social Science.

The Times (July 20, 1904)
in a leading article, said:

In the paper read on Monday at a meeting of the Sociological Society by Professor GEDDES—an abstract of which we print—are contained ideas of practical value to be recommended to the study of ambitious municipalities.   This is the age of cities, and all the world is city-building.   Almost everywhere is a flow from the country town-ward.   China and India may be still, in the main, lands of villages.   But the West, Russia perhaps excepted, is more and more peopled by dwellers in cities.   In a dim sort of way many persons understand that the time has come when art and skill and foresight should control what so far has been left to chance to work out; that there should be a more orderly conception of civic action; that there is a real art of city-making, and that it behoves this generation to master and practise it.   Professor Geddes truly said the land is already full of preparation as to this matter; the beginnings of a concrete art of city-making are visible at various points.   But our city rulers are often among the blindest to these considerations; and nowhere probably is to be seen a municipality fully and consistently alive to its duties in this respect.   London may be left out of the question.   Still a province rather than a city in the strict sense, wanting what, in the view of the early master of political science, was an essential of the true city, that it could "easily be overseen," with a vast floating population, it will be some time before it can be dealt with as an organic whole.   But the rulers of such communities as Manchester and Newcastle and York ought long ago to have realised, much more than has been done, that they are not so much brick and mortar, so much rateable area, so many thousands of people fortuitously brought together.   They have all a regional environment of their own which determined their origin and growth.   They have all a rich past, the monuments of which, generally to be found in abundance by careful, reverent inquirers, ought to be preserved; a past which ought to be known more or less to all the dwellers therein, and the knowledge of which will make the present more interesting.   Even when old buildings have disappeared, ancient roads, pathways, and streets can be traced; place names keep alive much history; and the natural features reveal to the practised eye what must have been the look and condition of a town in past ages.   Professor Geddes gives a sketch of what he conceives the vast and ever-growing literature of cities will one day be.   Even if the comprehensive monographs which he fore-shadows are never |140| written, it is not surely fanciful to expect that, with education universal, almost every dweller in our old towns will acquire some sort of that feeling with which a member of an ancient family looks upon its ancestral house or lands—will, even without much reading, have some sort of notion of his predecessors and a certain pride in his membership of an ancient community.   If he has not the good fortune to be a De Vere, a De Bohun, a Howard, Mowbray or Cavendish, he may perhaps be a citizen of a town which flourished when some of these families were unknown.

Such pride, or, as the lecturer preferred to term it, such "growth of civic consciousness and conscience, the awakening of citizenship towards civic renascence," will be the best security for a worthy city of the future.......

Professor Geddes glanced at the opening civic future, "the remoter and higher issues which a city's indefinitely long life and corre-spondingly needed foresight and statesmanship involve," the pos-sibilities which may be easily realised if only there be true civic pride, foresight, and unflagging pursuit of a reasonable ideal.......   It remains to be seen what our cities will become when for some generations the same spirit of pride and reverence shown by old families as to their possessions has presided over all civic changes and developments.......   Ruskin somewhere points out the mediaeval love of cities, unwholesome, dirty, and forbidding though they were. He did not teach his generation that that affection might with more reason attach to the modern city if its people knew what it had been and steadily strove to make it better, if there was in every large community patriotism and a polity.

Dr. J. H. BRIDGES in *The Positivist Review* (Sept., 1904), said: Under the title, "Civics, as applied Sociology," Prof. Geddes read on July 18th a very interesting paper before the Sociological Society. The importance of the subject will be contested by none. The method adopted in handling it, being in many ways original, invites remark.......

What is wanted is first a survey of the facts to be dealt with—a regional survey. This point of view has next to be correlated with corresponding practical experience acquired by practical civic life, but "aiming at a larger and more orderly conception of civic action."...... Students of Comte will not forget his well-known maxim, *Savoir pour prevoir, afin de pourvoir.*

What is to be the area of survey? Prof. Geddes decides that the City may be taken "as the integrate of study." Whether any modern towns, and, if so, what, may be taken as integrates in the sense which would undoubtedly apply to ancient Athens or to mediaeval Florence, may be questioned; but it is too soon to interrupt our author....... Every one who heard the lecturer must have been fascinated by his picture of a river system which he takes for his unit of study; the high mountain tracts, the pastoral hill-sides, the hamlets and villages in the valleys, the market town where the valleys meet, the convergence of the larger valleys into a county town, finally, the great city where the river meets the sea. The lecturer went on to advocate the systematic study of some of the principal river-basins of the world for the purpose of examining the laws which govern the grouping of cities. All would agree that much instruction might be derived from such |141| a survey, provided two dangers be avoided. One is the exaggeration of the influence of the environment on the social organism, an error into which the Le Play school have sometimes fallen; as when, for instance, it was sought to explain Chinese civilisation by the rice-plant. The other danger, which needs much care and thought to avoid, is the accumulation of such a mass of irrelevant detail as renders (perhaps sometimes it is intended to render) all generalisation impossible. Thinking men are at last beginning to regard the accumulation of memoirs as one of the principal obstacles to scientific progress. On the pretext of "more evidence," conclusions are adjourned, not merely *sine die*, but *sine spe diei*.   Yet so long as man is man, he must, and will, have conclusions; be they final or otherwise.

From the physiography of the city we pass to its history.....
In this part of his subject he has, as we all know, many precursors and fellow-workers.   The remarkable series, entitled "Historic Towns," instituted by Prof. Freeman, is known to most. The study of towns was the life and soul of Mr. Green's historic labours. Eloquent and powerful pictures of the great cities of the world fill the greater part of Mr. Harrison's well-known volume, "The Meaning of History"; and the student of universal history (a few of these, it may be hoped, are still left) finds them very stimulating and helpful.   The special note of Prof. Geddes' method is that he does not limit himself to the greater cities, but also, and perhaps by preference, deals with the smaller, and with their physical environ- ment; and, above all, that he attempts not merely to observe closely and thoroughly, but to generalise as the result of his observation. In biology, the study of any single organism, however minute and accurate, could reveal no laws (*i.e.*, no general facts) of structure or function.   As for instance, many forms of heart must be examined before the laws governing blood-circulation could be revealed; so here.   Countless, indeed, are the forms of cities; even limiting our field of observation to those that have grown up in the last century they are numerous enough.   Their differences and analogies would doubtless repay analysis, always supposing that we are clear how far the modern town, as contrasted with the mediaeval or Graeco- Roman city, can usefully be treated as "an integrate."   This raises large questions of nation, of groups of nations, finally of Humanity, which cannot here be touched.

Meantime, from the teacher's standpoint, there can be no question at all, among those who look upon education as something more than a commercial asset, as to the utility of looking on every old town, with the neighbourhood around it, as a condensed record, here and there perfect, elsewhere lamentably blotted, yet still a record, of the history of our race.   Historic memories survive in our villages far more widely than is thought.   The descendants of the man who found the body of Rufus in the New Forest still live hard by.   The builder whom the first William set to build Corfe Castle was Stephen Mowlem; and the Dorsetshire firm of Mowlem still pave London causeways.   A poor woman in a remote hamlet, untouched by tourist or guide-book, has shown me the ash-tree under which Monmouth was seized after Sedgemoor; a Suffolk peasant, equally innocent of book-knowledge, has pointed Out "Bloody Mary's lane," through which that bugbear of Protestants passed three hundred years before on her way to Framlingham. The abbey immortalised in Carlyle's "Past and Present," and still the wonder of Eastern England, is surrounded now by the same villages that Jocelyn tells us of.   The town named after St. Alban, with its memories of Cassivellaun and Julius Caesar, of an old Roman city, of the Diocletian persecution, of the great King Offa, founder of the abbey that was to become |142| at once a school of historical research, and our best epitome of mediaeval architecture—all this, with the monument of the author of the "Novum Organum" crowning the whole—sums up for us sixteen centuries of history.

Professor Geddes for more than twenty years has adopted this method of teaching sociology in the open air; "in the field," as geologists would say......

This is much more than the study and the description of buildings and places of historical interest.   His aim is first to study the way in which a city grows, always having due regard to its physical environment; secondly, by comparing like with like, as a naturalist compares the individuals of a species, or the species of a genus, to throw light on the laws which govern civic development, and thus to help forward and direct civic action.

All this is set forth with greater fulness in the Report which Professor Geddes has been asked to write for the Carnegie Dunfermline Trust.   The purpose of the Report (printed, but not yet published) was to suggest the way in which the revenue of the Trust, amounting to £25,000, should be spent for the benefit of this ancient and historic town.   The scheme, with its many pictures, real and ideal, of workshops, parks, culture-institutes—physical, artistic, and historical—will deeply interest even those who reject much of it as Utopian.   But it is at least a Utopia specially adapted to a given place and time, one in which every feature of landscape and history is made the most of, one in which a beginning can be made at once, leaving room for further developments as occasion may serve.   Moreover, it is penetrated through and through with the Republican ideal of bringing the highest truth within the reach of all.

Comte has pointed out, in the fifth chapter of his "General View of Positivism," and elsewhere, that it is not enough to enunciate sound principles of social renovation unless they can be rendered visible and palpable." "The principal function of art," he says, "is to construct types on the basis furnished by Science. . . . . . . However perfectly the first principles of social renovation may be elaborated by thinkers, they will still not be sufficiently definite for the practical results. . . . . . .   But, at the point where Philosophy must always leave a void, Art steps in, and stimulates to practical action. . . . . . .   Hence, in the future, systematic formation of Utopias will become habitual; on the distinct understanding that as in every other branch of art, the ideal shall be kept in subordination to the real."

Now, the Dunfermline Report is an admirable example of art thus allied with science for social service.   It is an ideal picture, strictly adherent to local colour and conditions, of an ancient city prolonging its vitality into the present and future by providing a very high form of training for its citizens, a training not of intellect only, but of the senses, of manual dexterity, of imagination, of Republican sympathy—a training in which "laborious inacquaintance with dead languages," infusing into the few touched by it a tincture of caste and militarism, gives way to comprehensive study of the evolution of Man, preparing the whole, and not a section merely, of the new generation for social service.

Such a Utopia as this may be looked upon as fulfilling the true social function of Art; standing midway between theory and practice; inspired by thought, and stimulating action. Only the social artist has to look to it that his thoughts be not merely true but adequate, lest he degenerate into a mere decorator.   How far will a series of "regional surveys," like those of |143| Mr. Booth in London and Mr. Rowntree in York, carry us!   Not so far, I fear, as Professor Geddes seems to hope.   Cities in our modern life are organs inseparable from a larger whole, the nation; and before the life of cities can be much changed, we have to ask ourselves, What is the national life?   What is its ethical and religious standard?   What is its practice as to the acquisition and distribution of wealth?   And, again, What is to be the intercourse of nations?   Is it to be war or peace?

Mr. Carnegie has given half a million for the benefit of a town

of 30,000 inhabitants.   Magnificent as the donation is, it is not too
much; not nearly enough, indeed, for the full realisation of Professor
Geddes' scheme.   Still, wisely used, it might accomplish great
results.   What we have recently sunk in the work of suppressing
two free States in South Africa would have made it possible to do
for three hundred towns what has been done for Dunfermline.   Half
of what we are now spending on our army and navy would enable
us to endow thirty more of such towns annually.

Mr. ISRAEL ZANGWILL in *To-day* (Aug. 10, 1904), said:

The Sociological Society is forging ahead at American speed; the
professors jostle one another, and Geddes treads on the heels of
Galton.   After "Eugenics," or the Science of Good Births, comes
"Civics," or the Science of Cities.   In the former Mr. Galton was
developing an idea which was in the air, and in Wells.   In the
latter Professor Geddes has struck out a more novel line, and a still
more novel nomenclature.   Politography, Politogenics, and Eu-
Politogenics, likewise Hebraomorphic and Latino-morphic and
Eutopia—quite an opposite idea from Utopia—such are some of the
additions to the dictionary which the science of Civics carries in its
train.   They are all excellent words—with the double-barrelled
exception—and still more excellent concepts.   But I fancy the
general idea of them all could be conveyed to the man in the street
under the covering of "the human shell."   This shell of ours is the
city.   It is the protective crust we have built round ourselves.   In
a smaller sense our house is our shell, but in a larger sense each
house is only a lobe of the complex and contorted whole.   Geography
shapes our shells from without, and the spirit of our particular
community shapes it from within.   History tells us how it has been
shaped in the past, Art tells us how it should be shaped in the
future.   Professor Geddes, in fact, envisages our civic shell as
becomes a brilliant biologist, who also happens to be a man of
historic imagination, ethical impulses, and aesthetic perceptions.
For the human shell is not merely geometrical and architectural,
like those of apian or beaverish communities; it holds and expresses
all those differences by which we are exalted above the bee or the
beaver.   It is coloured with our emotions and ideals, and contorted
with all the spirals of our history.   And all these manifestations

of humanity may be studied as systematically as those of the lower orders of creation, which have till recently monopolised the privilege of pin and label.   The old lady who admired the benevolence of Providence in always placing rivers by the side of large towns was only expressing in an exaggerated way the general failure to think of Civics scientifically.   The geographers, in whom may be found the bases of the science, have always pointed out that the river system is the essential unit for investigation.   From source to sea goes the line of evolution.   And yet even the peasant hamlet at the source depends, as |144| Professor Geddes reminds us, on the hinterland of pasture, forest, and chase; and the hunter is the germ of the soldier and the aristocrat.   The whole region contributes to the ultimate city, as the whole river to the ultimate sea.   The Professor says, justly enough, that we should try to recover the elemental or naturalist point of view, even for the greatest cities.   He sees London as "fundamentally an agglomeration of villages with their surviving patches of common around a mediæval seaport."   This is accurate vision; but when he discerns "even in the utmost magnificence of Paris, say, its Place de l'Etoile, its spread of boulevards, but the hunter's tryst by the fallen tree, with its radiating forest rides, each literally straight," I cannot help suspecting the over-ingenuity of a prolific intellect.   The view of London as a growth from embryos, and the view of Paris as the outcome of atavistic instinct, belong to different planes of scientific thinking.   That Haussmann in reconstructing Paris was merely an unconscious hunter and woodlander, building as automatically as a bee, is a fantastic hypothesis; since cities, if they are to be built on a plan at all, cannot avoid some unifying geometrical pattern; and there are not very many possibilities......   In the department of Eu-Politogenics we shall be confronted with the problem of consciously overriding what evolution has unconsciously evolved, and building towards a fairer future.   No doubt much of our creation will be imitation, and Professor Geddes is particularly suggestive in bidding us, at least, to be aware which of the tangled strands of influence we desire to follow; but a measure of artistic free-will remains.   With the development of a corporate conscience we should be able to turn out far more satisfactory shells than many that have blundered into being.   "Garden City" is only a particular application of the science of Civics.......

Eu-Politogenics concerns itself, however, with more than the mere configuration of our human shell.   Its colour and the music it holds are considerations no less important.   But they are too important to touch at the fag-end of an article.   Professor Geddes must, however, be congratulated on a stimulating paper, and upon his discovery of Eutopia.   For Eutopia (unlike Utopia, which is really Ou-topia, or no place) is merely your own place perfected. And the duty of working towards its perfection lies directly upon *you*.   "Civics—as applied sociology" comes to show you the way.

CIVICS: AS CONCRETE AND APPLIED
SOCIOLOGY, PART II
BY PROFESSOR GEDDES

Read before the Sociological Society at a Meeting in the School of Economics
and Political Science (University of London), Clare Market, W.C., on
Monday, January 23rd, 1905, the Rt. Hon. CHARLES BOOTH, F.R.S., in the
Chair.

A–INTRODUCTION: THE NEED OF CIVIC SURVEYS

To the previous discussion of this subject*the first portion of this
present title, "Civics as Concrete Sociology," would have been more
suitable than the second, (that of "Civics as Applied Sociology")
actually used.   For its aim was essentially to plead for the concrete
survey and study of cities, their observation and interpretation on
lines essentially similar to those of the natural sciences.   Since
Comte's demonstration of the necessity of the preliminary sciences
to social studies, and Spencer's development of this, still more since
the evolution theory has become generally recognised, no one
disputes the applicability of biology to |58| sociology.   Many are,
indeed, vigorously applying the conceptions of life in evolution, in
geographical distribution and environment, in health and disease,
to the interpretations of the problems of the times; while with the
contemporary rise of eugenics to the first plane of interest, both
social and scientific, these lines of thought, bio-social and bio-
geographic, must needs be increasingly utilised and developed.

But Comte and Spencer, with most other biologically-minded
sociologists have been more at home among biological generalisations and theories than among the facts they arise from, and hence
it is ever needful to maintain and extend a first-hand contact with
these.   I seek, therefore, to press home the idea that just as the

*"Sociological Papers," Vol 1., pp. 103–118.

biologist must earn his generalisations through direct and first-hand acquaintance with nature, so now must the sociologist work for his generalisations through a period of kindred observation and analysis, both geographic and historical; his "general laws" thus appearing anew as the abstract of regional facts, after due comparison of these as between region and region.

May not much of the comparative sterility of post-Comtean (or at any rate post-Spencerian) sociology, which is so commonly reproached to us, and to which the difficult formation and slow growth of sociological societies and schools is largely due, be thus explained?   Is it not the case that many able and persuasive writers, not only knowing the results, but logically using the generalisations of Comte or Spencer, as of old of Smith or now-a-days of List in the economic field, are yet comparatively sterile of fresh contributions to thought, and still more to action?   In fact, must we not apply to much of the literature of recent sociology, just as to traditional economics, the criticism of Comte's well-known law of three states, and inquire if such writers, while apparently upon the plane of generalised science, are not really in large measure at least arrested upon Comte's "metaphysical stage," Mill's "abstractional" one?

Conversely, the revival of sociological interest in this country at present is obviously very largely derived from fresh and freshening work like that of Mr Francis Galton and of the Right Hon. Charles Booth especially.   For here in Mr. Galton's biometrics and eugenics is a return to nature, a keen scrutiny of human beings, which is really an orderly fruition of that of the same author's "Art of Travel."   Similarly, Mr. Booth's "Survey of London" is as truly a return to nature as was Darwin's Voyage, or his yet more far-reaching studies in his garden and farmyard at home.

|59| Is it not the main support of the subtle theorisings and far-stretched polemic of Prof. Weismann that he can plague his adversaries with the small but literal and concrete mice and hydroids and water fleas with which his theories began?   And is it not for a certain lack of such concrete matter of observation that the vast systematisations of M. de Greef, or M. de Roberty, or the original and ingenious readings of Prof. Simon Patten leave us too often unconvinced, even if not sometimes without sufficiently definite understanding of their meaning?   The simplest of naturalists must

feel that Comte or Spencer, despite the frequently able use of the generalisations of biology, themselves somewhat lacked the first-hand observation of the city and community around them, and suffered thereby; this part of their work obviously not being on a level with the historic interpretations of the one or the psychological productivity of the other.   And if, without warlike intent, I may yet strike a conspicuous shield or two within these friendly lists, is it not this one element of concrete observation and illustration which is sometimes lacking to give its full effect to the encyclopaedic learning and the sympathetic insight of one of our recent papers, to the historic and poetic interpretations of another, or to the masterly logic of a third?

Before the polemics of our educationists, the voluminous argu-mentation and casuistic subtlety of our professors of economics and ethics, yet more before the profound speculations of the epistemol-ogists, the mere naturalist observer can but feel abashed like the truant before his schoolmasters; yet he is also not without a certain deep inward conviction, born of experience, that his outdoor world is yet more real, more vast, and more instructive than is theirs. And this impression becomes strengthened, nay verified and estab-lished, when he sees that the initiative thinkers from whom these claim to descend, have had in each and every case no merely academic record, but also a first-hand experience, an impulse and message from life and nature.   Hence the contributions of Locke, of Comenius, and of Rousseau.   Hence the Physiocrats found economics in peasant life; and thus too Adam Smith renewed their science, with due academic logic, doubtless, but from his experience of Glasgow and Kirkcaldy manufactures and trade.   Even the idealist Berkeley owed much of his theory to his iridescent tar-water; while surely the greater ethicists are those who have not only been dialecticians, but moral forces in the world of men.

In such ways, then, I would justify the thesis that civics is no abstract study, but fundamentally a matter of concrete and descrip-tive sociology—perhaps the greatest field of this.   Next, that such orderly study is in line with the preliminary sciences, and with the general doctrine of evolution from simple to complex; and finally with the general inquiry into the influence of geographical conditions on social development. |60| In short, the student of civics must be first of all an observer of cities; and, if so, of their origins and developments, from the small and simple beginnings of which the tiniest hamlet is but an arrested germ.   The productive sociologist should thus be of all investigators a wandering student *par excellence*; in the first place, as far as possible, a literal tourist and traveller—and this although like the homely Gilbert White or the world voyaging Darwin, he may do his best work around his own home.

B–INITIAL METHODS OF CONCRETE SURVEY

Hence our civic studies began (vol. 1, p. 105) with the survey of a valley region inhabited by its characteristic types—hunter and shepherd, peasant and fisher—each on his own level, each evolving or degenerating within his own region.   Hence the concrete picture of such a typical valley section with its types of occupation cannot be brought too clearly before our minds.*

What now of the causes of progress or decay? Are not these first of all the qualities and defects inherent in that particular social formation?—though we must also consider how these different types act and react, how they combine with, transform, subjugate, ruin or replace each other in region after region.   We thus re-interpret the vicissitudes of history in more general terms, those of the differentiation, progress or degeneracy of each occupational and social type, and the ascending and descending oscillations of these types.   In short, these occupational struggles underlie and largely interpret even the conflict of races, upon which Mr. Stuart-Glennie and other sociologists have so ably insisted.   The fundamental importance of these initial factors of region and occupation to all studies of races and types, of communities and institutions, of customs and laws, indeed of language and literature, of religion and art, even of ideals and individualities, must be my excuse if I seem to insist, in season and out of season, upon |61| the services of Le Play as one of the main founders of sociology; and this not only (*a*) on account of his monographic surveys of modern industrial life—those "Monographies Sociales" from which our current economic studies of the condition of the worker, of the family budget, etc., descend—but (*b*) yet more on account of his vital reconstruction of anthropology (albeit still far from adequately realised by most

*Fig. 1.

anthropologists) through his renewed insistence upon the elemental rustic origins of industry, family types, and social organisation alike, from these simplest reactions of man in his struggle for existence in varied and varying environment.

It does not suffice to recognise, with many economists, hunting, pastoral and agricultural formations, as states *preliminary* to our present industrial and commercial, imperial, and financial order of civilisation.   This view, still too commonly surviving, is rather of hindrance than help; what we need is to see our existing civilisation as the complex struggle and resultant of all these types and their developments to-day.   So far, therefore, from leaving, as at present, these simple occupational types to the anthropologist, or at best giving him some scant hospitality within our city museum, we are learning to see how it is at one time the eager miner, or the conservative shepherd, or at another the adventurous fisher or hunter who comes concretely upon the first plane of national, imperial or international politics, and who awakens new strife among these.   We not only begin to see, but the soldier frankly tells us, how the current sports of youth, and the unprecedented militarism of the past century, are alike profoundly connected with the hunting world.   Hence the hope of peace lies not only, as most at present think in the civilised and civilising development of international law, or of culture intercourse, excellent though these are, but also in a fuller and complete return to nature than has been this recent and persistent obsession of our governing classes with the hunter world almost alone; in short, in adding the gentler, yet wider, experiences of the naturalist, the sterner experiences of other occupations also.   Nor does such elementary recognition of these main social formations content us; their local differentiations must be noted and compared—a comprehensive regional survey, therefore, which does justice to each local vàriety of these great types; speaking henceforth of no mere abstract "hunter," but of the specific hunting types of each climate, and distinguishing these as clearly as do our own milder sportsmen of deer-forest and the turnip field from themselves and from each other. After such needed surveys in detail, we may, indeed must, compare and generalise them.

Similarly for the pasture, the forest.   Every tourist in this country is struck by the contrast of Swiss towns and cities with our own, and notes |62| too that on the Swiss pasture he finds a horde of cattle, while in Scotland or Yorkshire he left a flock of sheep. And not only the tourist, but the historian or the economist too often fail to see how Galashiels or Bradford are developments of the wool hamlet, now familiar to many in R. L. Stevenson's native Swanston. Again, not only Swiss wealth, but Swiss character and institutions, go back essentially to the high pasture and the well-filled byre. That this rich Swiss cow-pasture rests on limestone, and the poor Scottish sheep-grazing upon comparatively unmouldering and impermeable gneiss, is no mere matter of geologist's detail; it affords in each case the literal and concrete foundation-stone of the subsequent evolution of each region and population, and this not only in material and economic development, but even in higher and subtler outcomes, aesthetic, intellectual and moral.* It is for such reasons that one must labour and re-labour this geographic and determinist aspect of sociology, and this for no merely scientific reason, but also for practical ones. Nowhere perhaps have more good and generous souls considered how to better the condition of their people than in Swiss, or Irish, or Scottish valleys; yet it is one main reason of the continual failure of all such movements, and of such minds in the wider world as well, that they do not first acquaint themselves with the realities of nature and labour sufficiently to appreciate that the fundamental—I do not say the supreme— question is: what can be got out of limestone, and what can be got out of gneiss? Hence the rare educative value of such a concrete sociological diagram and model as was the Swiss Village at the Paris Exposition of 1900, for here geographic and economic knowledge and insight were expressed with artistic skill and sympathy as perhaps never before. Only as similar object-lessons are worked out for other countries, can we adequately learn, much less popularly teach, how from nature comes "rustics," and from this comes civics. But civics and rustics make up the field of politics; they are the concrete of which politics become the abstract— commonly the too remotely abstract.

For final illustration, let us descend to the sea-level. There again, taking the fisher, each regional type must be traced in his contribution to his town. Take for instance the salmon fisher of Norway, the whaler of Dundee, the herring-fisher of Yarmouth, the

*For a fuller justification of this thesis as regards Switzerland, see the writer's "International Exhibitions," in *International Monthly*, October, 1900.

cod-fisher of Newfoundland, the coral fisher of the Ægean; each is a definite varietal type, one developing or at least tending to develop characteristic normal family relations, and corresponding social outcomes in institutions; in which again the appropriate qualities and defects must be expressed, even as is the quality and twist of the hemp in the strength of the cable, or as is the chemistry and the microscopic structure of the alloy in the efficiency of the great gun.
|63| Our neighbouring learned societies and museums geographical, geological and the rest, are thus avowedly and consciously so many winter shelters in which respective groups of regional surveyors tell their tales and compare their observations, in which they meet to compare their generalisations from their own observations made in the field with those made by others.   So it must increasingly be for this youngest of societies.   We may, we should, know best our Thames valley, our London basin, our London survey; but the progress of our science implies as increasingly varied and thorough an inquiry into rustic and civic regions and occupations and result- ants throughout the whole world present and past, as does the corresponding world survey with our geologic neighbours.

I plead then for a sociological survey, rustic and civic, region by region, and insist in the first place upon the same itinerant field methods of notebook and camera, even for museum collections and the rest, as those of the natural sciences.   The dreary manuals which have too long discredited those sciences in our schools, are now giving place to a new and fascinating literature of first-hand nature study.   Similarly, those too abstract manuals of civics which are at present employed in schools* must be replaced by concrete and regional ones, their abstract counsels of political or personal perfection thus also giving place to a corresponding regional idealism which may then be supplemented from other regions as far as needs demand and circumstances allow.

C–GEOGRAPHICAL DETERMINISM AND ITS DIFFICULTIES

To interpret then our tangle of ideas, both of the city and its citizens, let us now bring more fully to our transverse valley sections, and to each occupation separately, the geographical view-point which we have found of service to elucidate the development of towns and

*For a fuller review of these, compare the writer's "City Development," in *Contemporary Review*, October, 1904.

cities upon its longi- |64| tudinal slope.   But this is neither more nor less than the method of Montesquieu, whose classic "Esprit des Lois" anticipates and initiates so much of that of later writers—Ritter, Buckle, Taine, or Le Play.   Once more then let their common, or rather their resultant, doctrine be stated in terms expressing the latest of these more fully than the first.   Given the region, its character determines the nature of the fundamental occupation, and this in turn essentially determines the type of family.   The nature and method of the occupation must normally determine the mode of its organisation, *e.g.*, the rise and character of a specialised directive class, and the nature of these occupational chiefs as contrasted with the people and with each other.   Similarly, the types of family tend to develop their appropriate types of institutions, *e.g.*, for justice, guidance, and of course notably in response to social environment as regards defence or attack.

Thus at this point in fact we seem to be pressing upon the student of sociology the essential argument of geographical and evolutionary determinism, in fact inviting him to adopt a view, indeed to commit himself to a method, which may be not only foreign to his habits, but repugnant to his whole view of life and history.   And if able advocacy of this determinist view of society for at least the past five generations has not carried general conviction, why raise so controversial a suggestion, in the guise too of a method professing to harmonise all comers?   Yet this is advisedly done; and as no one will deny some civil importance to geographical factors, let patience be granted to examine this aspect of the city's map and shield, and to get from it what it can teach, under the present assurance to the philosophic and idealist critic that his view of other factors, higher and deeper, as supreme in human life, and therefore in city making, will not be forgotten, nor excluded from consideration when we come to them.   All that is really insisted upon here is that if anything of naturalistic method of evolutionary conception is to be permitted at all, we must obviously proceed from this simple towards the more complex, and so begin with it here and now.

It is the appropriate slope or steppe, the needful rainfall, that conditions the growth of grass, this which conditions the presence of herds or flocks, and these again which determine the very existence of shepherds.   These granted then, not only do the pastoral arts and crafts arise, but the patriarchal type and family develop, and this not only with their hospitality and other virtues, with their nomadic tendencies, at any rate, their unfixed land-tenure, very different from the peasant's, but their slow and skilful |65| diplomacy (till the pasture is bared or grown again, as the negotiator's interests incline). The patriarch in his venerable age, the caravaneer in his nomadic and exploring youth, His disciplined maturity, thus naturally develop as different types of chief and leader; and it is therefore not until this stage, when all is ready for the entry of Abraham or Job, of Mohammed the camel-driver, or Paul the tent-maker, that any real controversy can arise between the determinist and his opponent, between the democratic and the great-man theories of history, towards which these respectively incline.*   And at that stage, may not the controversy stimulate a fruitful analysis?   After all, what is the claim of free-will but to select among the factors afforded by a given set of circumstances? And the utmost stretch of determinism to which geography and civics may lead us obviously cannot prove the negative of this. But whether the psychologic origins of new ideals be internal to the mind of genius, or imparted by some external source, is a matter obviously beyond the scope of either the geographer or the historian of civics to settle.   Enough surely for both controversialists if we use such a means of tabulating facts as to beg the question for neither view; and still better if we can present the case of each without injustice to either, nay, to each with its clearness increased by the sharp edge of contrast.   If the geographical determinist thesis on one hand, and its ethical and psychological antithesis on the other, can thus clearly be defined and balanced, their working equilibrium is at hand, even should their complete synthesis remain beyond us.

D–NEED OF ABSTRACT METHOD FOR NOTATION AND FOR INTERPRETATION

Not only such general geographical studies, but such social inter-pretations as those above indicated have long been in progress: witness the labours of whole schools of historians and critics, among whom Montsquieu and his immediate following, or in more recent times Buckle and Taine, are but the most prominent; witness the

---

*A fuller study, upon this method, of the essential origins of pastoral evolution, and of its characteristic modern developments, will be found in the writer's "Flower of the Grass," in *The Evergreen*, Edinburgh and Westminster, 1896.   See also "La Science Sociale," *passim*, especially in its earlier vols. or its number for Jan. 1905.

works of geographers like Humboldt, Ritter, Reclus, or of developmental technologists like Boucher de Perthes and regional economists like Le Play.   The main lines of a concrete and evolutionary sociology (or at |66| least *sociography*) have thus been laid down for us; but the task now before us, in our time, in such a society as this—and indeed in such a paper as the present one—its that of extracting from all this general teaching its essential scientific method, one everywhere latent and implicit, but nowhere fully explicit, or at least adequately systematised.

It is in fact only as we can agree upon some definite and orderly method of description that our existing literature of social surveys can be adequately compared or new ones co-operatively undertaken.   Hence the importance of discussions of scientific method such as those who have so largely occupied our first volume.   Yet, I submit, here lies the means of escaping from these too abstract (and consequently too static) presentments of the general methodology of social science into which sociologists are constantly falling; and to which must be largely ascribed the prevalent distaste for sociology so general in this would-be practical-minded community in which we find ourselves, as indeed also the comparative unattractiveness of our studies to the body of specialist scientific workers, not even excepting those within what we consider sociological fields.

The history of each science, be it mathematics or astronomy, botany, zoology or geology, shows us that it is not enough to have the intelligent observer, or even the interpretative thinker with his personally expressed doctrine.   This must be clearly crystallised into a definite statement, method, proposition, "law" or theory, stated in colourless impersonal form before it is capable of acceptance and incorporation into the general body of science.   But while astronomer and geologist and naturalist can and do describe both the observational results and their general conceptions in literary form, requiring from the ordinary reader but the patience to master a few unfamiliar terms and ideas, they also carry on their work by help of definite and orderly technical methods, descriptive and comparative, analytic and synthetic.   These, as far as possible, have to be crystallised beyond their mere verbal statement into formulae, into tabular and graphic presentments, and thus not only acquire greater clearness of statement, but become more and more active agencies of inquiry—in fact, become literal *thinking-*

machines.   But while the mathematician has his notations and his calculus, the geographer and geologist their maps, reliefs and sections, the naturalist his orderly classificatory methods, it has been the misfortune and delay of political economy, and no small cause of that "notorious discord and sterility" with which Comte reproached it, that |67| its cultivators have so commonly sought to dispense with the employment of any definite scientific notations; while even its avowed statisticians, in this country especially, have long resisted the consistent use of graphic methods.

I submit, therefore, for discussion, as even more urgent and pressing than that of the general and abstract methodology of the social sciences, the problem of elaborating a concrete descriptive method readily applicable to the study and comparison of human societies, to cities therefore especially.   To do justice to this subject, not only the descriptive labours of anthropologists, but much of the literature of sociology would have to be gone through from the "Tableau Economique" of the Physiocratic School to the "Sociological Tables" of Mr. Spencer, and still more fruitfully to more recent writers.   Among these, besides here recognising specially the work of Mr. Booth and its stimulus to younger investigators, I would acknowledge the helpful and suggestive impulse from the group of social geographers which has arisen from the initiative of Le Play,* and whose classification, especially in its later forms,† cannot but be of interest and value to everyone whose thought on social questions is not afloat upon the ocean of the abstract without chart or bearings.

Yet with all respect to each and all these classifications and methods, indeed with cordially acknowledge personal obligation and indebtedness to them from first to last, no one of these seems fully satisfactory for the present purpose; and it is therefore needful to go into the matter afresh for ourselves, though utilising these as fully as we can.

E–THE CITY-COMPLEX AND ITS USUAL ANALYSIS

In the everyday world, in the city as we find it, what is the working classification of ideas, the method of thought of its citizens?   That

*La Nomenclature Sociale (Extrait de La Revue, "La Science Sociale," Dec. 1886) Paris, Firmin-Diact, 1887.

†Demoulins, La Science Sociale d'apres F. Le Play 1882-1905; Classification Sociale, "La Science Sociale," Jan. 1905.

the citizens no more think of themselves as using any particular sociological method than did M. Jourdain of talking prose does not really matter, save that it makes our observation, both of them and it, easier and more trustworthy.

They are speaking and thinking for the most part of |68| People and of Affairs; much less of places.   In the category of People, we observe that individuals, self and others, and this in interest, perhaps even more than in interests, commonly take precedence of groups. Institutions and Government are, however, of general interest, the state being much more prominent than is the church; the press, for many, acting as the modern substitute for the latter.   In the world of Affairs, commerce takes precedence of industry, while sport runs hard upon both.   War, largely viewed by its distant spectators as the most vivid form of sport, also bulks largely.   Peace is not viewed as a positive ideal, but essentially as a passive state, at best, of non-war, more generally of latent war.   Central among places are the bank, the market (in its financial forms before the material ones).   Second to these stand the mines then the factories, etc.; and around these the fixed or floating fortresses of defence.   Of homes, that of the individual alone is seriously considered, at most those of his friends, his "set," his peers, but too rarely even of the street, much less the neighbourhood, at least for their own sake, as distinguished from their reaction upon individual and family status or comfort.

This set of views is obviously not easy of precise analysis of exact classification.   In broad outline, however, a summary may be made, and even tabulated as follows:—

THE EVERYDAY TOWN AND ITS ACTIVITIES.

PEOPLE	AFFAIRS	PLACES
(a) INDIVIDUALS (Self and others).	(a) COMMERCE INDUSTRY, etc. SPORT.	(a) MARKET, BANK, etc. FACTORY, MINE, etc.
(b) GOVERNMENT(S) Temporal and Spiritual (State and Church).	(b) WAR and Peace (Latent War).	(b) FORT, FIELD, etc.

Next note how from the everyday world of action, there arises a corresponding thought-world also.   This has, |69| of course, no less numerous and varied elements, with its resultantly complex local colour; But a selection will suffice, of which the headings may be printed below those of the preceding scheme, to denote how to the objective elements there are subjective elements corresponding—literal reflections upon the pools of memory—the slowly flowing stream of tradition.   Thus the extended diagram, its objective elements expressed in yet more general terms, may now be read anew (noting that mirror images are fully reversed).

	PEOPLE	AFFAIRS	PLACES
"TOWN"	(a) INDIVIDUALS	(a) OCCUPATIONS	(a) WORK-PLACES
	(b) INSTITUTIONS	(b) WAR	(b) WAR-PLACES
"SCHOOLS"	(b) HISTORY ("Constitutional")	(b) STATISTICS and HISTORY ("Military")	(b) GEOGRAPHY
	(a) BIOGRAPHY	(a) ECONOMICS	(a) TOPOGRAPHY

Here then we have that general relation of the town life and its "schools," alike of thought and of education, which must now be fully investigated.

Such diagrammatic presentments, while of course primarily for the purpose of clear expression and comparison, are also frequently suggestive—by "inspection," as geometers say—of relations not previously noticed.   In both ways, we may see more clearly how prevalent ideas and doctrines have arisen as "reflections upon" the life of action, and even account for their qualities and their defects—their partial truth or their corresponding inadequacy, according to our own appreciative or depreciative standpoint.   Thus as regards "People," in the first column we see expressed briefly how to (a) the individual life, with the corresponding vivid interest in biography, corresponds the "great man theory" of history. Conversely with (b) alone is associated the insistance upon institutional developments as the main factor.   Passing to the middle column, that of "Affairs," we may note in connection with (b) say the rise of statistics in association with the needs of war, a point connected with its too empiric character; or note again, a too common converse weakness of economic theory, its inadequate induc- |70| tive verification.   Or finally, in the column of "Place," the long weakness of geography as an educational subject, yet is periodic renewal upon the field of war, is indicated.   We might in fact continue such a comparison of the existing world of action and of ideas, into all the schools, those of thought and practice, no less than those of formal instruction; and thus we should more and more clearly unravel how their complexity and entanglement, their frequent oppositions and contradictions are related to the various and warring elements of the manifold "Town" life from which they derive and survive.   Such a fuller discussion, however, would too long delay the immediate problem—that of understanding "Town" and its "School" in their origins and simplest relations.

F–PROPOSED METHODICAL ANALYSIS.
(1) THE TOWN

More fully to understand this two-fold development of Town and School we have first of all apparently to run counter to the preceding popular view, which is here, as in so many cases, the precise opposite of that reached from the side of science.   This, as we have already so fully insisted, must set out with geography, thus literally *replacing* People and Affairs in our scheme above.

Starting then once more with the simple biological formula:

ENVIRONMENT. . . . CONDITIONS. . . . ORGANISM

this has but to be applied and defined by the social geographer to become

REGION. . . . OCCUPATION. . . . FAMILY-type and
Developments

which summarises precisely that doctrine of Montesquieu and his successors already insisted on.   Again, in but slight variation from Le Play's simplest phrasing ("*Lieu, travail, famille*") we have

PLACE. . . . . WORK. . . . . FOLK

It is from this simple and initial social formula that we have now to work our way to a fuller understanding of Town and School. |71| Immediately, therefore, this must be traced upward towards its complexities. For Place, it is plain, is no mere topographic site. Work, conditioned as it primarily is by natural advantages, is thus really first of all *place-work*. Arises the field or garden, the port, the mine, the workshop, in fact the *work-place*, as we may simply generalise it; while, further, beside this arise the dwellings, the *folk-place*.

Nor are these by any means all the elements we are accustomed to lump together into Town. As we thus cannot avoid entering into the manifold complexities of town-life throughout the world and history, we must carry along with us the means of unravelling these; hence the value of this simple but precise nomenclature and its regular schematic use. Thus, while here keeping to simple words in everyday use, we may employ and combine them to analyse out our Town into its elements and their inter-relations with all due exactitude, instead of either leaving our common terms undefined, or arbitrarily defining them anew, as economists have alternately done—too literally losing or shirking essentials of Work in the above formula, and with these missing essentials of Folk and Place also.

Tabular and schematic presentments, however, such as those to which we are proceeding, are apt to be less simple and satisfactory to reader than to writer; and this even when in oral exposition the very same diagram has been not only welcomed as clear, but seen and felt to be convincing. The reason of this difficulty is that with the spoken exposition the audience sees the diagram grow upon the blackboard; whereas to produce anything of the same effect upon the page, it must be printed at several successive stages of development. Thus our initial formula,

PLACE . . . . . WORK . . . . . FOLK

readily develops into

PLACE-WORK	WORK	FOLK
(Natural advantages)		FOLK-WORK
PLACE		(Occupation)

This again naturally develops into a regular table, of which the |72| filling up of some of the squares has been already suggested above, and that of the remaining ones will be' intelligible on inspection:—

Place folk ("Natives")	Work-folk ("Producers")	FOLK
Place-work	WORK	Folk-work
PLACE	Work-place	Folk-place

So complex is the idea of even the simplest Town—even in such a rustic germ as the "farm-town" of modern Scottish parlance, the *ton* of place-names without number.

The varying development of the Folk into social classes or castes night next be traced, and the influence and interaction of all the various factors of Place, Work, and Family tabulated. Suffice it here, however, for the present to note that such differentiation does take place, without entering into the classification and comparison of the protean types of patrician and plebeian throughout geography and history.

G—ANALYSIS CONTINUED.—(2) THE SCHOOL

Once and again we have noted how from the everyday life of action—the Town proper of our terminology—there arises the corresponding subjective world—the *Schools* of thought, which may express itself sooner or later in schools of education. The types of people, their kinds and styles of work, their whole environment, all become represented in the mind of the community, and these react upon the individuals, their activities, their place itself. Thus (the more plainly the more the community is a simple and an isolated one, but in appreciable measure everywhere and continually) there have obviously arisen local turns of thought and modes of speech, ranging from shades of accept and idiom to distinctive dialect or language. Similarly, there is a characteristic variety of occupational activity, a style of workmanship, a way of doing business. There are distinctive |73| manners and customs—there is, in short, a certain recognisable likeness, it may be an indefinably subtle or an unmistakably broad and general one, which may be traced in faces and costumes, in tongue and literature, in courtesy and in conflict, in business and in policy, in street and in house, from hovel to palace, from prison to cathedral.   Thus it is that every folk comes to have its own ways, and every town its own school.

While the complex social medium has thus been acquiring its characteristic form and composition, a younger generation has been arising.   In all ways and senses, Heredity is commonly more marked than variation—especially when, as in most places at most times, such great racial, occupational, environmental transformations occur as those of modern cities.   In other words, the young folk present not only an individual continuity with their organic predecessors which is heredity proper, but with their social predecessors also.   The elements of organic continuity, which we usually think of first of all as organic though of course psychic also, are conveniently distinguished as the *inheritance*—a term in fact which the biologist seeks to deprive of its common economic and social senses altogether, leaving for these the term *heritage*, material or immaterial alike.   This necessary distinction between the inheritance, bodily and mental, and the heritage, economic and social, obviously next requires further elaboration, and with this further precision of language also.   For the present, let us leave the term heritage to the economist for the material wealth with which he is primarily concerned, and employ the term *tradition* for these immaterial and distinctively social elements we are here specially considering.   This in fact is no new proposal, but really little more than an acceptance of ordinary usage.   Broadly speaking, tradition is in the life of the community what memory is for its individual units.   The younger generation, then, not only inherits an organic and a psychic diathesis; not only has transmitted to it the accumulations, instruments and land of its predecessors, but grows up in their tradition also.   The importance of imitation in this process, a matter of common experience, has been given the fullest sociological prominence, by M. Tarde especially.*   Thanks to these and other convergent lines

*Tarde, "L'Imitation Sociale," and other works.

of thought, we no longer consent to look at the acquirement of the
social tradition as a matter requiring to be imposed upon reluctant
youth almost entirely from without, and are learning anew as of
old, with the simplest and the most developed peoples, the barbarians
and the Greeks, to recognise and respect, and, if it may be, to
nourish the process of self-instruction, viewed as normal accom-
paniment of each developing being throughout the phases of its
|74| organic life, the stages of its social life.   Upon the many
intermediate degrees of advance and decline, however, between these
two extremes of civilisation, specific institutions for the instruction
of youth arise, each in some way an artificial substitute, or at least
a would-be accelerant, for the apprenticeship of imitation in the
school of experience and the community's tradition, which we term
a school in the restricted and pedagogic sense.   This whole discussion, however, has been in order to explain and to justify the present
use of the term "School" in that wide sense in which the historian
of art or thought—the sociologist in fact—has ever used the term,
while yet covering the specialised pedagogic schools of all kinds also.

Once more, then, and in the fullest sense, every folk has its own
tradition, every town its school.

We need not here discriminate these unique and characteristic
elements to which the art-historians—say of Venice and of Florence,
of Barbizon or Glasgow—specially attend from those most widely
distributed ones, in which the traditions and schools of all towns
within the same civilisation broadly agree.   Indeed, even the most
widely distributed of these—say from Roman law to modern antiseptic surgery—arose as local schools before they became general
ones.

Similarly for the general social tradition.   The fundamental
occupations and their division of labour, their differentiation in
detail and their various interactions up to our own day, at first
separately considered, are now seen to be closely correlated with the
status of woman; while all these factors determine not only the
mode of union of the parents, but their relation to the children, the
constitution of the family, with which the mode of transmission of
property is again thoroughly interwoven.

H—TOWN AND SCHOOL COMPARED

We may now summarise and tabulate our comparison of Town and

"TOWN"   FOLK

                    WORK

PLACE

SURVEY

            CRAFT-KNOWLEDGE

"SCHOOL"   CUSTOM

School,* and on the schema (p. 75) it will be seen |76| that each
element of the second is printed in the position of a mirror-reflection
of the first.   This gives but the merest outline, which is ready,
however, to be applied in various ways and filled up accordingly.
A step towards this is made in the next and fuller version of the
scheme (p. 77).   It will be noted in this that the lower portion of
the diagram, that of School, is more fully filled up than is the
upper.   This is partly for clearness, but partly also to suggest that
main elements in the origins of natural sciences and geography, of
economics and social science, are not always so clearly realised as
they might be.   The preceding diagram, elaborating that of Place,
Work, Folk (p. 75), however, at once suggests these.   Other features
of the scheme will appear on inspection; and the reader will find it
of interest and suggestiveness to prepare a blank schedule and fill
it up for himself.

These two forms of the same diagram, the simple and the more
developed, thus suggest comparison with the scheme previously
outlined, that of People, Affairs, Places (p. 68), and is now more
easily reconciled with this; the greater prominence popularly given
to People and Affairs being expressed upon the present geographic
and evolutionary scheme by the ascending position and more
emphatic printing (or by viewing the diagram as a transparency
from the opposite side of the leaf).

In the column of People, the deepening of custom into morals is
indicated.   Emphasis is also placed upon the development of law
in connection with the rise of governing classes, and its tendency
to dominate the standards previously taken as morals—in fact, that
tendency of moral law to become static law, a process of which
history is full.

---

*For the sake of brevity, an entire chapter has been omitted, discussing the
manifold origins of distinct governing classes, whether arising from the Folk, or
superimposed upon them from without, in short, of the contrast of what we may
broadly call patricians and plebeians, which so constantly appears through history,
and in the present also.   These modes of origin are all in association respectively
with Place, Work, and Family, or some of the various interactions of these.   Origin
and situation, migration, individual or general, with its conflict of races, may be
indicated among the first group of factors; technical efficiency and its organising
power among the second; individual qualities and family stocks among the third, as
also military and administrative aptitude, and the institutional privileges which so
readily arise from them.   Nor need we here discuss the rise of institutions, so fully
dealt with by sociological writers.   Enough for the present then, if institutions and
social classes be taken as we find them.

		GOVERNING CLASSES ∧ FAMILY TYPES
	INDUSTRIES	
REGION ¦ ∨	(WORK-PLACE)	(FOLK-PLACE) (TOWN)
∨ SURVEY !—LANDSCAPE ?—TERRITORY ¦ ∨	(CRAFT-TRADITION)	("SCHOOL") (FOLK-LORE)
∨ [NATURAL SCIENCES] ¦ ∨	[APPLIED SCIENCES]	[SOCIAL SCIENCES]
∨ GEOGRAPHY	ECONOMICS	CUSTOMS MORALS & LAWS

In the present as in the past, we may also note upon the scheme the different lines of Place, Work and Folk on which respectively develop the natural sciences, the applied or |78| technical sciences, and finally the social sciences, and the generalising of these respectively.

Thus, as we see the popular survey of regions, geography in its literal and initial sense, deepening into the various analyses of this and that aspect or element of the environment which we call the natural sciences—but which we might with advantage also recognise as what they really are, each a *geolysis*—so these sciences or geolyses, again, are tending to reunite into a higher geography considered as an account of the evolution of the cosmos.

Again, in the column of School, corresponding to Work, we have the evolution of craft knowledge into the applied sciences, an historic process which specialist men of science and their public are alike apt to overlook, but which is none the less vitally important.   For we cannot really understand, say Pasteur, save primarily as a thinking peasant; or Lister and his antiseptic surgery better than as the shepherd, with his tar-box by his side; or Kelvin or any other electrician, as the thinking smith, and so on.   The old story of geometry, as *"ars metrike,"* and of its origin from land-surveying, for which the Egyptian hieroglyph is said to be that of "rope stretching," in fact, applies far more fully than most realise, and the history of every science, of course already thus partially written, will bear a far fuller application of this principle.   In short, the self-taught man, who is ever the most fertile discoverer, is made in the true and fundamental school—that of experience.

The need of abbreviating the recapitulation of this, however, sooner or later develops the school in the pedagogic sense, and its many achievements, its many failures in accomplishing this, might here be more fully analysed.

Still more evident is this process in the column of Folk.   From the mother's knee and the dame's school of the smallest folk-place, the townlet or hamlet, *ton* or home, up to the royal and priestly school of the law of ancient capitals, or from the "humanities" of a mediaeval university to the "Ecole de Droit" of a modern metropolis, the series of essential evolutionary stages may be set down. Or in our everyday present, |79| the rise of schools of all kinds, primary, secondary, higher up to the current movement towards university colleges, and from these to civic and regional universities, might again be traced. The municipalisation of education is thus in fact expressed, and so on.

Leaving the schools in the main to speak for themselves of their advancing and incipient uses, a word may be said upon the present lines.

As a first and obvious application of this mode of geographic study of cities appears the criticism, and; when possible, the amendment of the city's plan, the monotonous rectangularity of the American city, and the petty irregularity more common in our own, being alike uneconomic and inartistic because ungeographic, irrational because irregional. With the improvement of communications, the physicist's point of view thus introduced—that of the economy of the energies of the community—is only beginning; the economy of fuel, the limitation of smoke and fogs being symptoms of this and pointing to a more economic organisation of industrial activities generally. But this next carries with it the improved efficiency of the producers themselves, with whom, however, the standpoint changes from the mere economisation of physical energies to the higher economy of organic evolution. The convention of traditional economics, that the productive capacity of the actual labourer is the sole concern of his science, thus gives place to what is at once the original conception of economics and the evolutionist one, viz., that the success of industry is ultimately measured neither by its return in wealth of the capitalist nor in money wages of the labourer, nor even by both put together, but in the results of industry upon the concrete environment, the family budget, the home, and the corresponding state of development of the family—its deterioration or progress. The organisation of industrial groups or of representative institutions found conducive to the well-being and progress of these prime civic units, the families, may now be traced into its highest outcome in city government. The method of analysis and graphic statement thus outlined may be shown to be even capable of useful application towards the statement of the best |80| arguments of both progressive and moderate parties in city politics.

Passing from Politics to Culture. Culture, the needs of this also become clearer; each community developing a similar general series of culture institutions, from the simplest presentation of its geography, landscape and architecture, to the complex development of industrial, technical and scientific instruction; and for provision also for the institutions of custom and ethic in school, law, and church.   Just as place, occupation, and family are intimately connected in the practical world, so their respective culture institutions must more and more be viewed as a whole.   Civic improvers will find their ideals more realisable as they recognise the complex unity of the city as a social development of which all the departments of action and thought are in organic relation, be it of health or disease.   The view of theoretic civics as concrete sociology, and of practical civics as applied sociology may be more simply expressed as the co-adjustment of social survey and social service, now becoming recognised as rational, indeed in many cities being begun.

I–DEVELOPMENT OF SCHOOL, AND ITS REACTION UPON TOWN

The reactions of the School upon the Town are observed in practice to be of very different values;—how are these differences to be explained?

From the very first the school is essentially one of memory, the impress of the town-life, even at its best and highest individual quality and impressiveness, as in the work of a great master, the observation and memory of which may long give his stamp to the work of his followers.   The fading of this into dulness, yet the fixing of it as a convention, is familiar to all in arts and crafts, but is no less real in the general lapse of appreciation of environment. Most serious of all is the fixation of habit and custom, so that at length "custom lies upon us with a weight heavy as death, and deep |81| almost as life."   This continual fixation of fashionable standards as moral ones is thus a prime explanation of each reformer's difficulty in making his moral standard the fashionable one, and also, when his doctrine has succeeded, of the loss of life and mummification of form which it so speedily undergoes.

Of conventional "education," considered as the memorisation of past records, however authoritative and classic, the decay is thus intelligible and plain, and the repetition of criticisms already adequately made need not therefore detain us here.

For this process is there no remedy?   Science here offers herself—with senses open to observe, and intellect awake to interpret.   Starting with Place, she explores and surveys it, from descriptive travel books at very various levels of accuracy, she works on to atlas and gazetteer, and beyond these to world-globe and "Geographie Universelle." With her charts and descriptions we are now more ready for a journey; with her maps and plans we may know our own place as never before; nay, rectify it, making the rough places plain and the crooked straight; even restoration may come within our powers.

Similarly as regards Work. Though mere empiric craft-mastery dies with the individual, and fails with his successors, may we not perpetuate the best of this? A museum of art treasures, a collection of the choicest examples of all times and lands, will surely raise us from our low level of mechanical toil; nay, with these carefully observed, copied, memorised, and duly examined upon, we shall be able to imitate them, to reproduce their excellencies, even to adapt them to our everyday work. To the art museum we have thus but to add a "School of Design," to have an output of more and less skilled copyists. The smooth and polished successes of this new dual institution, responding as they do to the mechanical elements of modern work and of the mechanical worker-mind, admitting also of ready multiplications as patterns, ensure the wide extension of the prevalent style of imitating past styles, designing patchwork of these; and even admit of its scientific reduction to a definite series of grades, which imitative youth may easily pass onwards from the age of rudest innocence to that of art-knowledge and certificated art-mastery. Our School of Design thus becomes a School of Art, a length a College, dominating the instruction of the nation, to the satisfaction not only of its promoters, but of the general public and their representatives, so that annual votes justly increase. Lurking discontent may now and then express itself, but is for practical purposes negligible.

|82| The example of art accumulation and art instruction is thus naturally followed in other respects. For the commercial information of the public, varied representative exhibitions—primarily, therefore, international ones—naturally suggest themselves; while so soon as expansion of imperial and colonial interests comes upon the first plane, a corresponding permanent Exhibition is naturally instituted. But when thus advancing commercial instruction, we must also recognise the claims of industry in all its crafts and guilds, and in fact the technical instruction of the community generally.

Hence the past, present, and promised rise of technical institutes
upon increasing scales of completeness.

In the rise of such a truly encylopaedic system of schools, the
university cannot permanently be forgotten.   Since from the outset
we have recognised the prime elements of the school in observation
and memory, the testing of these by examinations—written, oral,
and practical—however improvable in detail, must be fairly recognised, and the examining body or university has therefore to be
adopted as the normal crown of our comprehensive educational
system.   Teaching, however is found to be increasingly necessary,
especially to examination, and for this the main field left open is
in our last column, that of People.   Their lore of the past, whether
of sacred or classical learning, their history, literature, and criticism,
are already actively promoted, or at any rate adequately endowed
at older seats of learning; while the materials, resources, conditions
and atmosphere are here of other kinds.   Hence the accessibility
of the new University of London to the study of sociology, as yet
alone among its peers.

Hence, beside the great London, maritime, commercial and industrial, residential and governmental, there has been growing up,
tardily indeed, as compared with smaller cities, yet now all the more
massively and completely, a correspondingly comprehensive system
of schools; so that the historic development of South Kensington
within the last half century, from International Exhibitions of
Work, Natural History Museums of Place onwards to its present
and its contemplated magnitude, affords a striking exemplification
of the present view and its classification, which is all the more
satisfactory since this development has been a gradual accretion.

Enough then has been said to show that the rise of schools, their
qualities and their defects, are all capable of treatment upon the
present lines; but if so, may we not go farther, and ask by what
means does thought and life cope with their defects, especially that
fixation of memory, even at its best, that evil side of examination
and the like, which we often call Chinese in the bad sense, but which
we see arises so naturally everywhere?

|83|J–FROM "SCHOOL" TO "CLOISTER"

The preceding view is, as yet, too purely determinist.   The due
place of ideals, individual and corporate, in their reaction upon the

function and the structure of the city, and even upon its material environment, has next to be recognised.   For where the town merely makes and fixes its industry and makes its corresponding schools, where its habits and customs become its laws, even its morality, the community, as we have just seen, sinks into routine, and therefore decay.   To prevent this a twofold process of thought is ever necessary, critical and constructive.   What are these?   On the one hand, a continual and critical selection among the ideas derived from experience, and the formulation of these as Ideals: and further, the organisation of these into a larger and larger whole of thought; in fact, a Synthesis of a new kind.   This critical spirit it is which produced the prophets of Israel, the questioning of Socrates, and so on, to the journalistic and other criticism of life to-day. The corresponding constructive endeavour is now no mere School of traditional learning or of useful information.   It is one of science in a new and reorganised sense; one of philosophy also, one of ideals above all.

As from the Schools of the Law, as over against these, arise the prophets, so from the technical and applied sciences, the descriptive natural sciences, should arise the scientific thinkers, reinterpreting each his field of knowledge and giving us the pure sciences—pure geometry henceforth contrasted with mere land surveying, morphology with mere anatomy, and so on; while instead of the mere concrete encyclopaedia from Pliny or Gesner to Diderot or Chambers, vast subjective reorganisations of knowledge, philosophic systems, now appear.   Similarly, the mere observations of the senses and their records in memory become transformed into the images of the poet, the imagery too of the artist, for art proper is only thus born.   That mere imitation of nature, which so commonly in the graphic arts (though happily but rarely in music) has been mistaken for |84| art, thus modestly returns to its proper place—that of the iconography of descriptive science.

Thus from the Schools of all kinds of knowledge, past and present, we pass into the no less varied Cloisters of contemplation, meditation, imagination.   With the historian we might explore the Cloisters of the past, built at one time from the current ideals of the Good, at another of the True, at another of the Beautiful; indeed, in widely varying measures and proportions from all of these.   How far each of these now expresses the present, how far it may yet serve the future, is obviously a question of questions, yet for that very reason one exceeding our present limits.   Enough if in city life the historic place of what is here generalised under this antique name of Cloister be here recognised; and in some measure the actual need, the potential place be recognised also.   Here is the need and use, beyond the fundamental claims of the material life of the Town, and the everyday sanity of the Schools, with all their observations and information, their commonsense and experience, their customs and conventions, even their morals and their law, for a deeper ethical insight than any rule or precedent can afford, for a fuller and freer intellectual outlook than that which has been derived from any technical experience or empiric skill, for an imagery which is no mere review of the phantasmagoria of the senses.   In our age of the multiplication and expansion of towns, of their enrichment and their impoverishment, of the multiplication and enrichment of schools also, it is well for the sociologist to read from history, as he then may more fully see also around him that it is ever some fresh combination of these threefold products of the Cloister—ideal theory, and imagery—emotional, intellectual, sensuous—which transforms the thought-world of its time.

The philosopher of old in his academic grove, his porch, the mediaeval monk within his studious cloister's pale, are thus more akin to the modern scientific thinker than he commonly realises—perhaps because he is still, for the most part, of the solitary individualism of the hermit of the Thebaid, of Diogenes in his tub.   Assuredly, they are less removed in essential psychology than their derived fraternities, their |85| respective novices and scholars, have often thought.   It is thus no mere play of language which hands on from the one to the other the "travail de Bénédictin," though even here the phrase is inadequate savouring too much of the school, into which each cloister of every sort declines sooner or later, unless even worse befall.

The decay of the cloister, though thus on the one hand into and with the school, may also take place within itself, since imagination and ideal may be evil, and theory false.   That examples of all these decays abound in the history of religion, of philosophy, of art also, is a commonplace needing no illustration.   Nor should the modern investigator think his science or himself immune to the same or kindred germs in turn.

K–THE CITY PROPER

Now, "at long last," we are ready to enter the city proper.   This is not merely the Town of place and work and folk, even were this at their economic best.   It is not enough to add the School, even at its completest; nor the cloister, though with this a yet greater step towards the city proper is made.   For though this is not itself the City, its ideals of human relations, its theory of the universe and man, its artistic expression and portrayal of all these, ever sooner or later react upon the general view and conduct of life. Hence the Academe of Plato and the Lyceum of Aristotle, the mediæval cloister and the modern Research Institute, have been so fertile, so creative in their influence upon the city's life, from which they seemed to be retired.   Hence it is ever some new combination of the threefold product of the cloister—ideal, idea, and image—which transforms the world, which opens each new epoch. Each new revelation and vision, each system of thought, each new outburst of poetry and song, has moved the men of its age by no mere mechanical pressure of economic need or external force, by no mere scholastic instruction, but in a far subtler way, and into new and unexpected groupings, as the |86| sand upon Chladon's vibrating plate leaps into a new figure with each thrill of the violinist's bow.

Instead of simply developing our morals from custom, and therefore codifying them into law as in the school they are now boldly criticised, as in part if not in whole, hindrances to a better state of things.   As this becomes more and more clearly formulated as an ideal, its ethic transcendence of convention and law not only becomes clear, but the desire for its realisation becomes expressed.   This may be with all degrees of clearness of reason and vividness of imagery, yet may remain long or altogether in the plane of literature, as has Plato's Republic or More's Utopia—standard and characteristic types of the cloister library as we may call it, one of inestimable value to the world in the past, and perhaps in our time needed as much as ever to help us to see somewhat beyond the output of the busy presses of town and school.   Yet our ideal, our "Civitas Dei," "Civitas Solis," need not remain unrealised: it may be not only seriously planned towards realisation, as was Platonopolis of old, but bravely founded, as has been done in cases without number, from the ancient world to modern communities, by no means wholly unsuccessful.   Though in our great industrial towns, our long

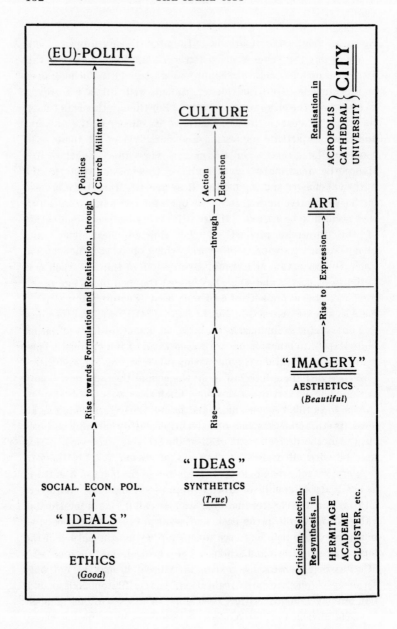

settled regions, such new departures seem less easy, the principle remains valid—that it is in our ideal of polity and citizenship, and in our power of realising this, that the city proper has its conception and its birth.   Again, instead of simply deriving our thought from experience we now project our clarified thought into action and into education; so that from cloister of philosophy, and from its long novitiate of silence, there grows up the brotherhood of culture, the culture city itself.   Similarly in art, we no longer imitate nature, nor copy traditional designs.   Art proper appears, shaping bronze and marble into images of the gods, and on a burnt and ruined hill-fort renewing the Parthenon.   In general terms, instead of simply adjusting, as in the school, our mental picture to the outward facts, we reverse the process; and with a new art conception, be it good or bad, we transform the outward world, like wax under the seal. Thus from the |88| cloister and chapel of the musician, the studio-cell of the artist, the scriptorium of the poet, comes forth the architect, remodelling the city around his supreme material expression and home of its moral and material reorganisation, its renewed temporal and spiritual powers.   Of this, the city proper, the Acropolis of Athens, the Temple of Jerusalem, the Capitol and Forum of Rome are classic and central examples, and in the mediæval city, pre-eminently the cathedral; though beside this we must not forget the town house and its belfry, the guild houses, the colleges, the great place, the fountains, the city cross, and if last, still best if good at all, the streets and courts and homes.   Returning once more to the history of educational development, we have here a means of unravelling the apparently perplexing history of univers-ities.   For the university past or present has but its foundations in the school, with its local and its general tradition, whatever may be the accordance of these with well-ascertained fact, its true novitiate can only be afforded in the cloister of reflection and research, of interpretation and synthesis; while for its full devel-opment it needs the perpetual renewal of that generous social life—that inspiring intercourse "of picked adolescents and picked senescents"—which has marked the vital periods of every university worthy of the name.

   In summary then, to the town has been added the school, with its advantages, its increasingly obvious limitations also, which it is for the cloister to remedy—even the advantages of the barrack

TOWN			SCHOOL
	PLACE	SURVEY	
WORK		KNOWLEDGE	
FOLK		MORALS	LAW
POLITY		SOC. ECON. IDEALS ETHICS	
	CULTURE	IDEAS	
CITY	ART	IMAGERY	CLOISTER

finding a main element of its claim in this no less than in its professed training as regards citizenship.   But here also it is for few to remain, albeit free for each to return at will.   Ideals, to survive, must surely live, that is, be realised; hence for full life one needs "to meditate with the free solitary; yet to live secular, and serve mankind."

L–THE CITY COMPLETED: TOWN, SCHOOL, CLOISTER, AND CITY PROPER

In course of this fourfold analysis, it is plain that we have reached the very converse—or at all events the comple- |90|ment—of that geographical determinism with which we started, and that we have returned to a view corresponding to the popular one (of "People, Affairs, Places," p.69), which we then set aside for the reasons given.   The "great man theory" of history, at best less crudely stated, thus reappears; in short, to the initial thesis we have now the distinct antithesis.   It is time, therefore, to bring these together towards the needed synthesis.   Hence to the page (p. 77) on which was summarised the determinist view of Town and School, we now require the complemental statement upon page (p. 87 of Cloister and City proper.   Nor must we be content, with too many controversialists hitherto, to keep in view only one at a time; but by folding back the pages of print between these two half-schemes, as the book lies open, to take in both together.

We may thus finally compress the essentials of this whole paper into a simple formula—

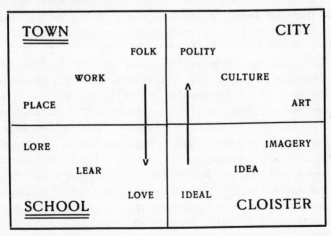

or most briefly—

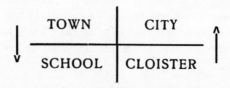

|91|—noting in every case the opposite direction of the arrows.   The application of this formula to different types of town, such as those already indicated in the former instalment of this paper (Vol. I., p. 107) or in the present one, will not be found to present any insuperable difficulty.   It must, however, be kept clearly in view that the city of each day and generation subsides or decays more or less completely into the mere town anew, as the cloister into the schools.   The towns and cities of the world are thus classifiable in terms of their past development and present condition.

Summary

Condensing now this lengthy, yet compressed and abbreviated series of analyses into a single page of summary, we may briefly define the main aspects and departments of civics from the present point of view.   First then, comes the study of civics as fundamentally (and ever anew) an orderly development—at once geographic, economic, and anthropologic in its nature—a survey of place, work, and folk—and these not merely or mainly as broken up into the fine dust of censuses and statistics, nor even of the three too separate sciences above named, but as a living unity, the human hive, the Town.

Corresponding to this objective and organic life we reorganise its fundamental subjective life.   This is fundamentally, and ever partially, the record and reflex of the life of the hive, the Town: of all its general and particular environment and function, its family type and development; and however overlaid by imported culture or by decayed ideals, it is fundamentally expressed in local knowledge, in craft tradition, in kinship and its associated kindness, in habits and customs, and their developments up to morals and laws.   Simple terms corresponding to place, work, and folk, are hard to find; say, however, till better be suggested, that in close relation to the maternal arms in which general social thought and its utmost pedagogic developments alike begin, it is place-lore, work-lear, and folk-love, which are the essentials of every |92| School.* That existing educational machineries may not adequately recognise these is not of course the question here.

These three terms, lore, lear, and love are thus well related to their respectively deepening levels of sense, intelligence and feeling; and their respective relation is thus more plain to the imagery, the theory, and the idealism above defined as the essentials of the Cloister. The psychology of the processes of poetic, philosophic and spiritual awakening and renewal is in these days being approached anew, both from the individual and social side, but cannot here be entered upon.

Finally and supremely arises the City proper—its individuality dependent upon the measure and form in which ideals are expressed and harmonised in social life and polity, ideas synthetised in culture, and beauty carried outwards from the study or chamber of the recluse into the world of art.

Practical conclusion

The investigation of the City thus tends towards the practice of citizenship.   Thus social survey prepares for social service, as diagnosis towards treatment and hygiene; and these react fruitfully upon our knowledge and understanding anew.   Beyond social observations, and the needed observatories for making them more adequately, we need social activities and the laboratories for preparing them, or at least the leavens of them; or, again, in happier phrase, at once simple and more synthetic, we need some shelter†

*The use of *lore* as primarily empirical, and derived from the senses, it is traditional; it is well therefore to restrict it to this, and to revive the old word *lear*, still understood in Scotland in these precise senses—intellectual, rational, yet traditional, occupational also.

†Without forgetting the many institutions and workers in almost all departments of the field of civics, the rise of definite surveys and of scientific groupings like this Society, without ignoring also the many admirable workers and institutions of social endeavour, and their progressive integration into Social Unions, Institutes of Service, and the like, I may be permitted to press for the need of uniting both types, the scientific and the practical, into a single one—a civic museum and active centre in one.   Of this type, my own Outlook Tower at Edinburgh is, so far as I am aware, the earliest beginning; and, despite its rudimentary condition, may thus serve to suggest a type of institution which will be found of service alike to the sociologist and the citizen.

into which to gather the best |93| seed of past flowerings and in which to raise and tend the seedlings of coming summers. We need definitely to acquire such a centre of survey and service in each and every city—in a word, a Civicentre for sociologist and citizen.

M–THE HISTORIC CITY-COMPLEX

The criticism may have already arisen in the reader's mind that the "Town" and "School" of our analysis are by no means so simple as we have assumed them. Our surveys of antique towns ever disclose the material survivals, at least the vestiges, of the cloister or the acropolis of the past, of its cathedral or its forum. The processes of our industries, in what is now their daily artisan routine, include, repeat, condense, what were yesterday or longer ago living inventions, each instinct with Promethean fire. The hackneyed ornament of our homes was once glowing with beauty, radiant or dark with symbolism. So it is for our everyday customs and institutions, and so for living languages; our own, perhaps, most of all. These, of course, are facts made familiar by investigators of all orders, from the scholar and antiquary of old, the historian and philologist of yesterday, to the geographer or the sociologist of our own time: witness Mr. Spencer's masterly treatment of their main results. How, then, shall we correlate this process of all things growing old with the analysis of cities above attempted?   In other words, how shall we interpret the course of their historic evolution, their renewed growth and decay, progress and degeneracy, their present condition, crowded with residues of the past, with those potentialities which our outline discloses?   This is the more necessary since this fourfold analysis applies in principle to all human groupings from the simplest village to the Eternal City.   To this, indeed, we have in principle already traced it, onwards from our primitive valley section with its humble hamlets, its fundamental occupations.

Returning then to our main diagram, with its four-fold analysis of the City so soon as we have completed this, and |94| carried its progress up to the level of city life proper, we must next turn over the leaf and begin a new page, with place and work and folk once more.   This simplest of acts expresses with graphic significance the very process of history; for in closing our diagram page its

"Cloister" has been folded down on the "School," our cathedral and forum, our "City" proper upon the "Town." Thus it is that the ideals and the achievements of one day and generation and city are ever melting away, and passing out of sight of the next; so that to the joy or sorrow of the successors the new page seems well nigh bare, though ever there comes faintly through some image or at least blurred suggestion of the fading past. Hence each page of history is a palimpsest. Hence our modern town, even when yesterday but prairie, was no mere vacant site, but was at once enriched and encumbered by the surviving traditions of the past; so that even its new buildings are for the most part but vacant shells of past art, of which now only the student cares to trace the objective annals, much less penetrate to the inner history. So for the decayed Renaissance learning of our schools, for the most part so literally dead since the "Grammarian's Funeral"; and so, too, for the unthinking routines, the dead customs and conventions, and largely too the laws and rituals of our urban lives. Hence, then, it is that for the arrest and the decay of cities we have no need to go for our examples to the ancient East. These processes, like those of individual senility and death, are going on everywhere day by day.

Upon the new page, then, it is but a complexer "Town" and "School" anew: we have no continuing City. This too commonly has existed at its best but for the rare generation which created it, or little longer; though its historic glories, like those of sunset and of after-glow, may long shed radiance and glamour upon its town, and linger in the world's memory long after not only these have faded, but their very folk have vanished, their walls fallen, nay their very site been buried or forgotten. Upon all these degrees of dying, all these faint and fading steps between immortality and oblivion, we may arrange what we call our historic cities. Obviously in the |95| deeper and more living sense the city exists only in actualising itself; and thus to us it is that the ideal city lies ever in the future. Yet it is the very essence of this whole argument that an ideal city is latent in every town. Where shall we in these days find our cloistered retreats to think out such ideals as may be applicable in our time and circumstances: the needed kinetic ethics, the needed synthetic philosophy and science, the needed vision and imagery and expression of them all?

N–THE EVILS OF THE CITY
Disease, defect, vice and crime

I have spoken little of town evils, and much of town ideals, primarily for the reason that even to recognise, much less treat, the abnormal, we must know something of the normal course of evolution. Hence, the old and useful phrase by which physiology used to be known, that of "the institutes of medicine."   Sociology has thus to become "the institutes of citizenship."

Often though philanthropists forget this, diagnosis should precede treatment.   The evils of the city, by the very nature of our hypothesis, demand special survey, and this no less thoroughly than do the normal place and work and industry.   It is only our most permanent intellectual impulse, that of seeking for unity, which excuses the cheap unitary explanations so often current; as, for instance, that social evils are mainly to be explained by intemperance, as for one school of reformers; by poverty or luxury, for a second and third; by Tammany or other form of party government, by socialism or by individualism for yet others; that they are due to dissent or to church, to ignorance or to the spread of science, and so on almost indefinitely—doubtless not without elements of truth in each!

Yet let me offer as yet another explanation of civic evils, this more general one—distinguished from the preceding by including them all and more—that not only is our "Town" in itself imperfect, but the other three elements we have been characterising as school, cloister and city, are yet more imperfect, since disordered, decayed, or undeveloped anew.   It is because of each and all of these imperfect realisations of our civic life, that the evils of life sink down, or flame out, into these complex eruptions of social evils with which our human aggregations are as yet cursed.

Hence, to those who are struggling with disease and pain, with ignorance and defect, with vice, and with crime, but for the most part too separately, it is time to say that all these four evils are capable of being viewed together, and largely even treated together.   They are not unrelated, but correspond each as the negative to that fourfold presentment of ideals we have hitherto been raising.   To this ideal unity of healthy town, with its practical and scientific schools of all kinds, with its meditative cloister of ethical and social idealism, of unified science and philosophy, of imagination and drama, all culminating in the polity, culture, and art which make a city proper, we have here the corresponding defects in detail.

The evils of existing city life are thus largely reinterpreted; and if so more efficiently combated; since the poverty, squalor and ugliness of our cities, their disease and their intemperance, their ignorance, dulness and mental defect, their vice and crime are thus capable not only of separate treatment but of an increasingly unified civic hygiene, and this in the widest sense, material and moral, economic and idealist, utilitarian and artistic.   Even the most earnest and capable workers towards civic betterment in these many fields may gain at once in hope and in efficiency as they see their special interests and tasks converging into the conception of the city as an organic unity, and this not fixed and settled, nor even in process of progress or degeneration from causes beyond our ken, but as an orderly development which we may aid towards higher perfection, geographic and cultural alike.

Our modern town is thus in a very real sense, one not hopeless, but as hopeful as may be, a veritable purgatory; that is a struggle of lower and higher idealisms, amid the respective expressions and outcomes of these.   Indeed, in our own present |97| cities, as they have come to be, is not each of us ever finding his own Inferno, or it may be his Paradise?   Does he not see the dark fate of some, the striving and rising hope of others, the redemption also?

The supreme poetic utterance of the mediaeval world is thus in great measure, as each thoughtful reader sees, an expression of impassioned citizenship and this at one of the golden moments of the long history of city life.   This expression—this exiled citizen's autobiographic thought-stream—is resumed at every level, from youthful home and local colour, from boyish love and hopes, from active citizenship and party struggle, to the transfiguration of all these.   Hence these mystic visions, and these world ambitions, temporal and spiritual; hence this rise from cloistered faith and philosophy into many-sided culture; hence the transformation of all these through intensest symbol-visions into enduring song.

Am I thus suggesting the *Divina Comedia* as a guide-book to cities?   Without doubt, though not necessarily for beginners.   Yet who can see Florence without this, though we may pack below it Baedeker and Murray?   Or who, that can really read, can open a volume of Mr. Booth's severely statistical Survey of London, with all its studious reserve, its scientific repression, without seeing between its lines the Dantean circles; happy if he can sometimes read them upward as well as down?

O–A CIVIC SYMBOL AND ITS MEANING

But such books of the city, whether of the new and observant type, from Baedeker to Booth, or of the old and interpretative Dantean one, are too vast and varied to keep open before us.   Even the preceding open page of diagram is complex enough with its two-fold, indeed four-fold city; and we are called back to our daily work in the first of these divisions, that of the everyday town.   Since its subjective aspects of school and cloister may fade from memory, its higher aspect also, that of city proper, how can we retain this four-fold |98| analysis, and how test if it be true?   Take then one final illustration; this time no mere logical skeleton, however simple or graphic, but an image more easily retained, because a concrete and artistic one, and moreover in terms of that form of life-labour and thought-notation—that of current coin—which, in our day espe-cially, dominates this vastest of cities; and hence inherits for the region of its home and centre—"the Bank" which has so thoroughly taken precedence of the town-house and cathedral, of the fortress and palace—the honoured name of "City."   The coinages of each time and place combine concrete and social use with statements of historic facts; and they add to both of these a wealth of emblematic suggestions: but that is to say, they express not only their town, and something of its *school*, but much of its thought also, its *cloister* in my present terminology.

So before me lies an old "bawbee" of my own home city.   On one side stands the hammerman at his anvil, below him the motto of his guild, "*Non marte sed arte*."   Here then the industrial "Town" and its "School" express themselves plainly enough, and precisely as they have been above defined.   But on the other side spreads the imperial double eagle; since Perth *(Bertha aurea)* had been the northmost of all Rome's provincial capitals, her re-named "Victoria" accordingly, as the mediaeval herald must proudly have remembered, so strengthened his associations with the Holy Roman Empire with something of that vague and shadowy historic dignity which the Scot was wont to value so much, and vaunt so high.   On the eagle's

breast is a shield, tressured like the royal standard, since Perth was
the national capital until the "King's Tragedy" of 1457; but instead
of the ruddy lion the shield bears the lamb with the banner of St.
John, the city's saint.   This side, too, has its motto, and one
befitting an old capital of King and Commons, both in continual
strife with the feudal nobles, "*Pro Rege, Lege, et Grege.*"   Here
then, plain upon this apparent arbitrarily levised trifle, this petty
provincial money-token, this poor bawbee, that is, this coin not
only of the very humblest order, but proverbially sordid at that, we
find clearly set down, long generations ago, the whole |99| four-fold
analysis and synthesis of civic life we have been above labouring
for.   For what makes the industrial Town, what can better keep
it than strenuous industry at its anvil?   How better express its
craft school, its local style and skill, its reaction too upon the town's
life in peace and war, than by this Hal o' the Wynd by his forge?
Nay, what better symbol than this hammer, this primitive tool and
ever typical one, of the peaceful education of experience, form
Prometheus to Kelvin, of the warlike, from Thor to modern cannon-
forge?   Turning now from Town and School to Cloister, to the life
of secluded peace and meditation—from which, however, the practical issues of life are ever renewed—what plainer symbol, yet what
more historic or more mystic one can we ask than this of the lamb
with the banner?   While of the contrasted yet complemental civic
life of fullest, broadest action, what expression like the Roman
eagle—the very eyes of keenness, and the spreading wings of power?

So rarely perfect then is this civic symbol, that I must not omit
to mention that it has only come to my notice since the body of this
paper, with its four-fold analysis of cities as above outlined, was
essentially finished.   Since it thus has not in any particular suggested the treatment of cities here advocated, it is the more
interesting and encouraging as a confirmation of it.   It is also to
my mind plain that in this, as in many other of our apparent
"advances in science," and doubtless those in social studies particularly, we are but learning to think things anew, long after our
forefathers have lived them, even expressed them—and these in
their ways no less clear and popular than can ever be ours.   That
we may also again live them is once more curiously expressed by
the same symbol; for its re-appearance is due to its having been
appropriately revived, in a fitting art form, that of the commem-

orative and prize medal of the local arts and crafts exhibition, held in the new Public Library, under civic auspices.   Little scrutiny of this last sentence will be needed to see the four-fold completeness of the civic event which it describes.

For just as we have seen on the old coin the hammer- |100| man and his motto answer to the town and school; so now on its reissue fo the renascent local arts and crafts, with their commemoration in this library.   And as the greater motto, that of widest policy, corresponds to the cloister of reflection and resolve, so we note that this new impulse to civic betterment is associated with the new library—no mere school-house of memory, but also the open cloister of our day.   Finally, note that this impulse is no longer merely one of aesthetic purpose, of "art for art's sake," nor its execution that of a cultured minority merely; it announces a re-union of this culture and art with the civic polity.   What fitter occasion, then, for the striking of a medal, than this renewal of civic life, with municipal organisation and polity, art and culture, renascent in unison.   That such events are nowadays far from exceptional is so true that we are in danger of losing sight of their significance.   Yet it is amid such city developments that the future Pericles must arise.

We thus see that our analysis is no mere structural one, made post-mortem from civic history; but that it applies to the modern functioning of everyday life in an everyday city, so soon as this becomes touched anew towards cultural issues.   Furthermore, it is thus plain that civic life not only has long ago anticipated and embodied our theories of it, but once more outruns them, expressing them far better than in words—in life and practice.   In this way the reader who may most resent these unfamiliar methods of exposition, alternately by abstract diagram or concrete illustration—which may seem to him too remote from ordinary life and experience, perhaps too trival—may now test the present theory of the city, or amend it, by means of the ample illustrations of the processes and results of social life which are provided by his daily newspaper, and these on well-nigh all its fields and levels.

Note finally that it is the eagle and lamb of temporal and spiritual idealism that form the "head" of this coin, the craftsman and anvil but the modest "tail."   The application is obvious.

Thus even numismatics revives from amid the fossil |101| sciences.   For from this to our own common coinage, or notably to that of France, America, Switzerland, etc., the transition is easy, and still better to that of the noblest civic past, both classic and mediæval. Without pursuing this further here my present point is gained, if we see, even in the everyday local details of work and people, the enduring stamp, the inextinguishable promise, of the flowering of our everyday industries and schools into worthier ideals than they at present express, and of the fruition of these in turn upon nobler heights of life and practice. It expresses the essential truth of the popular view of the city; that in terms of the formula—People..... Affairs..... Places—above referred to (page 69). It also explains the persistent vitality of this view, despite its frequent crudity, and lack of order in detail, in face of the more scientific treatment here at first employed, that in the elementary geographic order—Place.... Work.... People. For though this objective order be fundamental, it is the complementary subjective evolution which throughout history has ever become supreme; so that our scheme must combine the outward geographic presentment with the inward psychological one. This may be graphically expressed by changing the order of presentment from that used hitherto:—

$$\frac{\text{Town} \mid \text{City}}{\text{School} \mid \text{Cloister}} \quad to \quad \frac{\text{City} \mid \text{Town}}{\text{Cloister} \mid \text{School}}$$

P–FORECAST OF CITY DEVELOPMENT. SPECIAL AND GENERAL

The dual and four-fold development of the city, as above sketched, is by no means far advanced in most of our present towns or cities, which have obviously but scanty expression of the ideas shadowed forth for the modern equivalents of cloister and cathedral, of academe and acropolis. But this is to say that such towns, however large, populous and rich according to conventional economic standards, are to that extent small and poor, indeed too often little better than cities by courtesy. Yet their further development, upon this |102| four-fold view of civic evolution, though in principle the same for each and all, has always been, and let us hope may always be, in large measure an individual (because regional) one. For if each human individuality be unique, how much more must that of every city?

In one concrete case, that of Dunfermline, I have already submitted definite suggestions towards the realisation of the civic Utopia, and even architectural designs towards its execution,* so that these may at any rate suffice to show how local study and adaptive design are needed for each individual city, indeed for every point of it. It is thus, and thus only, that we can hope to have a city development truly evolutionary, that is, one utilising the local features, advantages, and possibilities of place, occupation, and people. Of course, it is needful to supplement these by the example of other cities; but it is no less needful to avoid weighting down the local life with replicas of institutions, however excellent elsewhere, if really irregional here. With the re-awakening of regional life in our various centres, and of some comprehension of its conditions among our rulers, they will cease to establish, say, a school of mines in Piccadilly, or again one of engineering and the like in South Kensington. The magistrates of Edinburgh have long abandoned their old attempt to plant mulberries and naturalise silk culture upon their wind-swept Calton Hill; albeit this was a comparatively rational endeavour, since a population of Huguenot refugee silk weavers had actually come upon their hands.

Similarly, it is plain that we must develop Oxford as Oxford, Edinburgh as Edinburgh, and so on with all other cities, great or small—York or Winchester, Westminster or London. And so with Chelsea or Hampstead, with Woolwich or Battersea. Has not the last of these grown from a mere outlying vestry, like so many others, into a centre of genuine vitality and interior progress, indeed of ever-widening interest and example; and all this in half a generation, apparently through the sagacious leadership—say, rather the devoted, the |103| impassioned citizenship—of a single man? And does not his popular park at times come near giving us a vital indication of the needed modern analogue of cathedral and forum? Civic development is thus no mere external matter, either of "Haussmannising" its streets, or of machine-educating its people; the true progress of the city and its citizenship must alike grow and flower from within albeit alive and open to every truly fertilising impulse from without.

Yet since national interests, international industry, commerce,

*Cf. the writer's "City Development," Edinburgh and Westminster, 1904.

science, and therefore progress are nowadays and increasingly so
largely one, may we not in conclusion foresee something at least of
the great lines of development which are common to cities, and
generalise these as we are accustomed to do in history?   Witness
the Classical, Mediæval, and Renaissance types to which historic
cities preponderatingly belong, and within which we group their
varied individualities, as after all of comparative detail.

Here then it is time to recall the presentment of ancient, recent
and contemporary evolution already outlined in the part of this
paper previously read (Vol. I, p. 109), dealing with the historic
survey of cities.   We have now to face the question, then postponed,
indeed left in interrogation-marks—that of seeking not indeed
sharply to define the future order of things, yet in some measure to
discern such elements of progress as may be already incipient in the
existing order, if not yet largely manifest there.   Such elements
may be reasonably expected to grow in the near future, perhaps
increasingly, and whatever be their rate of growth are surely worthy
of our attention.

Contemporary science, with its retrospective inquiries into origins
in the past, its everyday observation of the present, is apt practically
to overlook that the highest criterion and achievement of science
is not to decipher the past, nor record the present, not even to
interpret both.   It is to foresee: only thus can it subserve action,
of which the present task ever lies towards the future, since it is for
this that we have to provide.   Why then should not Comte's famous
aphorism—"*Voir pour prévoir, prévoir pour pourvoir*," become
applicable in our civic studies no less than in the general social and
political fields to |104| which he applied it?   In navigation or
engineering, in agriculture or hygiene, prevision and provision alike
are ever increasing; yet these are no mere combinations of the
preliminary sciences and the fundamental occupations, but obviously
contain very large social elements.

It is proverbially safe to prophesy when one knows; and it is but
this safe prediction which we make every day of child or bud, where
we can hardly fail to see the growing man, the coming flower.   Yet
do not most people practically forget that even now, in mid-winter,
next summer's leaves are already waiting, nay, that they were
conceived nine months ago?   That they thus grow in small, commonly unnoticed beginnings, and lie in bud for a period twice as

long as the summer of their adult and manifest life, is yet a fact, and one to which the social analogies are many and worth considering.

While recognising, then, the immense importance of the historic element of our heritage, renaissance and mediæval, classic and earlier; recognising also the predominance of contemporary forces and ideas, industrial and liberal, imperial and bureaucratic, financial and journalistic, can we not seek also, hidden under all these leaves, for those of the still-but-developing bud, which next season must be so much more important than they are to day?   It is a commonplace, yet mainly of educational meetings, to note that the next generation is now at school; but how seldom do we recognise its pioneers, albeit already among our own contemporaries?   At any rate we may see here and there that their leaven is already at work.

In this respect, cities greatly differ—one is far more initiative than another.   In the previous paper (vol. 1, p. 109), we saw how individuals, edifices, institutions, might represent all past phases; these, therefore, often predominate in different cities sufficiently to give its essential stamp.   Why then should we not make a further survey and seek to see something of the cities of the future; though we may have to look for these in quarters where at first sight there may seem as yet scanty promise of flower?

|105| To recall an instance employed above, probably every member of this Society is old enough to remember incredulous questionings of whether any good thing could come out of Battersea.   Again, how few, even in America, much less than in Europe, a few years ago, forsaw the rapid growth of those culture-elements in St. Louis, of which the recent World-Exposition will not have been the only outcome?

Only a few years earlier, it was Chicago which, for New England no less than for the Old World, seemed but the byword of a hopelessly materialised community.   So Birmingham or Glasgow has won its present high position among cities in comparatively recent times; so it may now be the turn of older cities, once far more eminent, like Newcastle or Dundee, to overtake and in turn, perhaps, outstrip them.   But all this is still too general and needs further definition; let us attempt this, therefore, somewhat more fully, in the concrete case of Glasgow.

Q–GLASGOW AS TYPICAL OF CIVIC TRANSITION—
FROM "PALEOTECHNIC" TO "NEOTECHNIC"

My own appreciation of the significance of Glasgow was first really awakened over twenty years ago by William Morris, who in his vivid way pointed out to me how, despite the traditional culture—superiority of Edinburgh, Glasgow was not only the Scottish capital, but, in his view, in real progressiveness the leading and initiative city of the whole United Kingdom. And this for him was not merely or mainly in its municipal enterprise, then merely in its infancy—although he expressed this development in the phrase "In London, people talked socialism without living it; but in Glasgow, they were socialists without knowing it!" Despite all the ugliness which had so repelled Ruskin, the squalor which moved Matthew Arnold to the fiercest scorn in all his writings, Morris's appreciation arose from his craftsman's knowledge and respect for supreme craftsmanship. The great ships building upon the Clyde were for him "the greatest achievement of |106| humanity since the days of the cathedral-builders," nay, for him actually surpassing these, since calling forth an even more complex combination and "co-operation of all the material arts and sciences" into a mighty and organic whole; and correspondingly of all their respective workers also, this being for him of the very essence of his social ideal.

For these reasons he insisted, to my then surprise that the social reorganisation he then so ardently hoped for "was coming faster upon the Clyde than upon the Thames": he explained as for him the one main reason for his then discouragement as to the progress of London that there East and West, North and South, are not only too remote each from the other, but in their occupations all much too specialised—there to finance, there to manufactures, or here to leisure, and so on; while on the Clyde industrial organisation and social progress could not but develop together, through the very nature of the essential and working unity of the ship.

Since Morris's day, a local art movement, of which he knew little, has risen to eminence, a foreign critic would say to pre-eminence, in this country at least. Since Ruskin's savage response to a Glasgow invitation to lecture—"first burn your city, and cleanse your river,"—a new generation of architects and hygienists have not a little transformed the one, and vigorous measures have been taken towards the purification of the other. That the city and university pre-eminently associated with the invention of the steam-engine, and consequently with the advent of the industrial revolution throughout the world, should, a century later, have produced a scarcely less pre-eminent leader of applied science towards the command of electricity is thus no isolated coincidence. And as political economy, which is ever the theory corresponding to our phase of industrial practice, and there some of its foremost pioneers, and later its classical exponent, Adam Smith himself, so once more there are signs at least of a corresponding wave of theoretic progress.

Students of primitive civilisation and industry have now long familiarised us with their reinterpretation of what was long known as the stone age, into two very distinct |107| periods, the earlier characterised by few and rough implements, roughly used by a rude people, the second by more varied tools, of better shape, and finer edge, often of equisite material and polish. We know that these were wielded more skilfully, by a people of higher type, better bred and better nourished; and that these, albeit of less hunting and militant life, but of pacific agricultural skill, prevailed in every way in the struggle for existence; thanks thus not only to more advanced arts, but probably above all to the higher status of woman. This distinction of Paleolithic and Neolithic ages and men, has long passed into the terminology of sociological science, and even into current speech: is it too much then, similarly, to focus the largely analogous progress which is so observable in what we have been wont to generalise too crudely as the modern Industrial Age? All are agreed that the discoveries and inventions of this extraordinary period of history constitute an epoch of material advance only paralleled, if at all, in magnitude and significance by those of prehistory with its shadowy Promethean figures. Our own advance from a lower industrial civilisation towards a higher thus no less demands definite characterisation, and this may be broadly expressed as from an earlier or *Paleotechnic* phase, towards a later or more advanced *Neotechnic* one. If definition be needed, this may be broadly given as from a comparatively crude and wasteful technic age, characterised by coal, steam, and cheap machine products, and a corresponding *quantitative* ideal of "progress of wealth and population"—towards a finer civilisation, characterised by the wider command, yet greater economy of natural energies, by the predominance of electricity, and by the increasing victory of an ideal of "qualitative progress, expressed in terms of skill and art, of hygiene and education, of social polity, etc.

The Neotechnic phase, though itself as yet far from completely replacing the paleotechnic order which is still quantitatively predominant in most of our cities, begins itself to show signs of a higher stage of progress, as in the co-ordination of the many industries required for the building of a ship, or in the yet more recent developments which begin to renew for us the conception of the worthy construction of a city. As |108| the former period may be characterised by the predominance of the relatively unskilled workman and of the skilled, so this next incipient age by the development of the chief workman proper, the literal *architectos* or architect; and by his companion the rustic improver, gardener and forester, farmer, irrigator, and their correspondingly evolving types of civil engineer.

To this phase then the term *Geotechnic* may fairly be applied. Into its corresponding theoretic and ideal developments we need not here enter, beyond noting that these are similarly of synthetic character; on the concrete side the sciences unifying as geography, and on their more abstract side as the classification and philosophy of the sciences,—while both abstract and concrete movements of thought are becoming more and more thoroughly evolutionary in character.

But evolutionary theories, especially as they rise towards comprehensiveness, cannot permanently content themselves with origins, or with classifications merely, nor with concentrating on nature rather than on man. Nature furnishes after all but the stage for evolution in its highest terms; of this man himself is the hero; so that thus our Geotechnic phase, Synthetic age (call it what we will) in its turn gives birth to a further advance—that concerned with human evolution, above all subordinating all things to him; whereas in all these preceding industrial phases, even if decreasingly, "things are in the saddle and ride mankind." This age, now definitely evolutionist in policy, as the geotechnic was in theory and in environment we may term the *Eugenic*. For its theory, still less advanced, the term *Eupsychic* may complete our proposed nomenclature.

Thus then our conception of the opening future may be increasingly defined, since all these apparently predicted phases are already incipient among us, and are thus really matters of observed fact, of social embryology let us say; in short, of city development.

In summary, then, the diagram of the former instalment of this paper (vol. 1, p. 109)

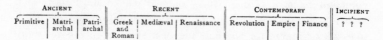

|Primitive| Matri-archal | Patri-archal ‖ Greek and Roman | Mediæval | Renaissance ‖ Revolution | Empire | Finance ‖ ? ? ?

ANCIENT			RECENT			CONTEMPORARY			INCIPIENT
Primitive	Matri-archal	Patri-archal	Greek and Roman	Mediæval	Renaissance	Revolution	Empire	Finance	? ? ?

|109| has thus its interrogations filled up. Omitting the left-hand half, that generalised as Ancient and Recent in the above diagram, so as to give more space to the Contemporary and Incipient phases, these now stand as follows:—

CONTEMPORARY			INCIPIENT		
Revolution	Empire	Finance	Neotechnic	Geotechnic	Eugenic

To elaborate this farther would, of course, exceed my present limits; but I may be permitted to say that long use of this schematic outline, especially of course in more developed forms, has satisfied me of its usefulness alike in the study of current events and in the practical work of education and city betterment. I venture then to recommend it to others as worth trial.

R–A PRACTICAL PROPOSAL—A CIVIC EXHIBITION

How shall we more fully correlate our theoretic civics, *i.e.*, our observations of cities interpreted as above, with our moral ideas and our practical policy—*i.e.*, our Applied Civics. Our ideals have to be selected, our ideas defined, our plans matured; and the whole of these applied; that is realised, in polity, in culture, and in art. But if this be indeed the due correlation of civic survey and civic service, how may we now best promote the diffusion and the advancement of both? At this stage therefore, I venture to submit to the Society a practical proposal for its consideration and discussion; and if approved, I would fain hope for its recommendation to towns and cities, to organisations and to the public likely to be interested.

Here then is my proposal. Is not the time ripe for bringing together the movements of Civics and Eugenics, now here and indeed everywhere plainly nascent, and of setting these before the public of this country in some such large and concrete ways, as indeed, in the latter subject at least, have been so strongly desiderated by Mr. Galton?   As regards Civics, such have been afforded to America during the summer of 1904 by the Municipal Section of the St. Louis Exhibition; in |110| Dresden also, at the recent Towns Exhibition; and by kindred Exhibitions and Congresses in Paris and elsewhere.

All these have taken form since the Paris Exposition of 1900, with its important section of social economy and its many relevant special congresses.   Among these may be specially mentioned here as of popular interest, and civic stimulus, the *Congrès de L'Art Public*; the more since this also held an important Exhibition, to which many Continental cities sent instructive exhibits.

Other exhibitions might be mentioned; so that the fact appears that in well-nigh every important and progressive country, save our own, the great questions of civics have already been fully opened, and vividly brought before their public, by these great contemporary museums with their associated congresses.

With our present Chairman, the Rt. Hon. Charles Booth, with Canon Barnett, Mr. Horsfall, and so many other eminent civic workers among us; with our committee and its most organising of secretaries, might not a real impulse be given in this way by this Society towards civic education and action?

Let me furthermore recall the two facts; first, that in every important exhibition which has been held in this country or abroad, no exhibits have been more instructive and more popular than have been (1) the picturesque reconstructions of ancient cities, and the presentment of their city life, and (2) the corresponding surveys of the present conditions of town life, and of the resources and means of bettering them.

Even as a show then, I venture to submit that such a "Towneries" might readily be arranged to excel in interest, and surpass in usefulness, the excellent "Fisheries," "Healtheries", and other successful exhibitions in the record and recent memory of London. The advantages of such an exhibition are indeed too numerous for even an outline here; but they may be easily thought out more and more fully.   Indeed, I purposely abstain for the present from more concrete suggestion; for the discussion of its elements, methods, plans, and scale will be found to raise the whole range of civic questions, and to set these in freshening lights.

|111| At this time of social transition, when we all more or less feel the melting away of old divisions and parties, of old barriers of sects and schools, and the emergence of new possibilities, the continual appearance of new groupings of thought and action, such a Civic Exhibition would surely be specially valuable.   In the interest, then, of the incipient renascence of civic progress, I plead for a Civic Exhibition.*

Of such an exhibition, the very catalogue would be in principle that *Encyclopaedia Civica*, into which, in the previous instalment of this paper (vol. 1, p. 118) I have sought to group the literature of civics.   We should thus pass before us, in artistic expression, and therefore in universal appeal, the historic drama of the great civic past, the mingled present, the phantasmagoria and the tragi comedy of both of these.   We should then know more of the ideals potential for the future, and, it may be, help onward some of the Eutopias which are already struggling towards birth.

---

*Since the preceding paper was read, it is encouraging to note the practical beginnings of a movement towards a civic exhibition, appropriately arising, like so many other valuable contributions to civic betterment, from Toynbee Hall.   The Cottages Exhibition initiated by Mr. St. Loe Strachey at Garden City, and of course also that admirable scheme itself, must also be mentioned as importance forces in the directions of progress and propaganda advocated above.

The Chairman (THE RT. HON. CHARLES BOOTH) said:
I feel always the inspiring character of Professor Geddes'
addresses.   He seems to widen and deepen the point of view, and
to widen and deepen one's own ideas, and enables us to hold them
more firmly and better than one can do without the aid of the kind
of insight Professor Geddes has given into the methods of his own
mind.   I believe that we all hold our conceptions by some sort of
tenure.   I am afraid I hold mine by columns and statistics much
underlined—a horrible prosaic sort of arrangement on ruled paper.
I remember a lady of my acquaintance who had a place for everything.   The discovery of America was in the left-hand corner; the
Papacy was in the middle; and for everything she had some local
habitation in an imaginary world.   Professor Geddes is far more
ingenious than that, and it is most interesting and instructive and
helpful to follow these charming diagrams which spring evidently
from the method he himself uses in holding and forming his
conceptions.   That it is of the utmost value to have large conceptions there can be no doubt—large conceptions both in time and
place, large conceptions of all those various ideas to which he has
called our attention.   By some means or other we have to have
them; and having got them, every individual, single fact has redou-
bled value.   We put it in its place.   So I hope that in our discussion,
while we may develop each in his own way, the mental methods we
pursue, we may bring forward anything that strikes us as germane,
as a practical point of application to the life of the world, and
especially anything having an application to the life of London.
I would make my contribution to that with regard to a scheme that
has been explained to me by its originator, Mrs. Barnett, the wife
of Canon Barnett of Toynbee Hall.   The idea concerns an open

|113| space which has recently been secured in Hampstead. It is known to you all that a certain piece of ground belonging to the trustees of Eton College has been secured, which extends the open space of Hampstead Heath in such a way as to protect a great amount of beauty. The further proposal is to acquire an estate surrounding that open space which has now been secured for ever to the people, and to use this extension to make what is called a "garden suburb." It is a following out of the "garden-city" idea which is seizing hold of all our minds, and it seems to me an exceedingly practical adaptation of that idea. Where it comes in, in connection with the address we have just heard, is that the root idea is that it shall bring together all the good elements of civic life. It is not to be for one class, or one idea, but for all classes, and all ideas—a mixed population with all its needs thought for and provided for; and above everything, the beauty of those fields and those hills is not to be sacrificed, but to be used for the good of the suburb and the good of London. I hope that out of it will come an example that will be followed. That is a little contribution I wish to make to the discussion to-day, and if I can interest any one here in forwarding it, I shall be exceedingly glad.

MR. SWINNY said:

Towards the close of his lecture, Professor Geddes remarked that the cities of America inherited a great part of their civilisation from Greece and Rome and the Europe of the Middle Age. I believe that thought will lead us to consider the point whether this geographical survey should precede or follow a general historical survey. Now, if we consider that a river valley in England, with the towns in that valley, are part of the English nation, and that the English nation has shared in the general historical evolution of Western Europe, it would seem that the first simplification the question allows of is: What is there in the historical development of that city that is common to the whole of Western Europe, and what is peculiar to its position as an English city? And the second simplification that the problem allows of is to consider what part of the evolution of a particular city is due to its peculiar position in that river valley? So that it seems necessary first to get a general idea of the historical evolution of England and the West; and then you can proceed to consider what is due to the part played by the city in that evolution. Thus you have to consider not so much the city as a result of its immediate environment, but the effect of its environment in modifying the general course of civilisation as it affected that city.

DR. J. L. TAYLER,

|114| referring to Professor Geddes' remarks on the working crafts-man and the thinking craftsman, said he believed that in a country like England, where the prevailing tendencies of thought and action were of an essentially practical nature, many people who now felt contempt for higher mental ideals would alter their views, if this idea of the *causal* relationship between thinkers and workers could be driven home. If business men and women could be made to realise that in the higher regions of pure science there were always to be found some thinkers who belonged to the same craft or trade as they themselves, they would naturally tend to rely on these thinkers when dealing with problems that necessitate a wide mental outlook.

Moreover, the thought that students of great mental powers studied the objects with which working craftsmen were in daily contact, could not fail to deepen, refine and purify their more practical and, in some respects, grosser aims; while the knowledge that every science-study had an industrial as well as a scientific aspect would make the thinking craftsmen more alive to the needs of everyday existence.

Such conceptions, if spread through all classes of our community, would inevitably change the feeling of distrust of learning into one of healthful enthusiasm, and give in addition a unity and direction to our various life pursuits which might in time generate a true modern national spirit; for it is precisely this divorce of mental and physical, of theoretical and practical, class and individual effort—which such a thinking and working craft theory would rectify—that destroys our efficiency by creating an unreal chasm between refined and unrefined, learned and unlearned, where there should be only a progressive evolution from the lower to the higher, from the immediate practical to the ultimate ideal.

THE REV. DR. AVELING said:

There was one point that the lecturer made which, I think, might be a fit and fruitful subject for discussion. He said that we were

the product of the city.   To a great extent that is undoubtedly
true; but on the other hand, he advocated an improvement in the
conditions of environment, to be brought about by our own endeavours.   Therefore, the city can be shaped and made by us.   What,
then, is the exact value to be given to the seemingly contradictory
doctrines that the individual is the product of the city and also that
the city is the product of the citizen?   The establishing of some
fixed relation between—or the adjusting of the relations of—these
two causes of social progress would be, I think, interesting to the
philosopher, and useful to the economist.   The problem is |115|
without doubt a difficult one, but its solution would be of great
value.   I do not venture to offer any answer to the question I
raise—I merely state it.

MR. A. W. STILL said:

We have been passing through a period in which the city has created
a type of man so wholly absorbed in the promotion of his own
individual interests that he tends almost entirely to forget the social
obligations which ought to make the greatest appeal to him.   We
may take some hope from what Professor Geddes has said, that the
time is coming when we shall bring the force of our own characters
to bear on our environment, and endeavour to break away from
conditions which have made us the slaves of environment.   I know
the lovely little garden city of Bourneville intimately, and some of
the experiments in other quarters.   But in the common expansion
of cities, I have seen that as the people get away from one set of
slums, they are creating new areas which will become as degraded
and abominable as those which are left behind.   It has always
seemed to me that there is room for good work by some committee,
or some body of men, who would be voluntary guardians of the
city's well-being, who would make it their business to acquire all
that knowledge which Professor Geddes has just put before us in
terms so enchanting, and would use all the ability that they possess
in order to lead the minds of the community towards the cultivation
of the best and highest ideals in civic life.   I do not think it need
be regarded as impossible that, from an association of this kind,
such a movement as I have mentioned should spring.   I conceive
the possibility of each group developing into a trust, capable of
acting in the interests of the city in years to come, exercising a

mighty influence, being relied upon for guidance, and administering great funds for the common good.   If we could get in each of our populous centres a dozen thoroughly intelligent broad-minded men, capable of watching all the streams of tendency—all the developments of civic life, bringing their judgment to bear on its progress, and urging the public to move in the right direction, a great service might be rendered.   At least once a year, these little groups of men might meet together at some general conference, and, by the exchange of their opinions and by the mutual helpfulness of intellectual intercourse, raise up and perfect civic ideals which would be a boon to this country.   We suffer at present, I think, from the too great particularisation of our efforts.   We get one man devoting himself exclusively to a blind asylum, another seeming to take no interest in anything but a deaf-and-dumb institute or the like, and yet another devoting himself to charity organisation.   It is all excellent work, but the difficulty is to get broad, comprehensive views taken of the common good.   To reduce poverty and to check physical degeneracy, there must be an effort continuously made to |116| raise the tone of the environment in which we live.   The home and the city need to be made wholesome and beautiful, and the people need to be encouraged to enlarge their minds by contact with nature, and by the study of all that is elevating and that increases the sum of social responsibility.

MR. E. S. WEYMOUTH said:

He found it somewhat difficult to see what was to be the practical outcome of civics if studied in the way proposed.   Would Professor Geddes consider it the duty of any Londoner, who wished to study sociology practically, to map out London, and also the surrounding districts, with special reference to the Thames River Basin, as appeared to be suggested in both Professor Geddes' papers?   Looking at civics in its practical or ethical aspect, he was bound to confess that, though he had acquired a tolerable knowledge of the geography of the Thames Basin, he did not feel it helped him materially towards becoming a better citizen of London.   Would Professor Geddes wish them to study, first, London with its wealth side by side with its squalor and filth, and then proceed to study another large town, where the same phenomena presented themselves?   What gain would there be in that proportionate to the

labour entailed?   In his own case, so disheartened had he felt by
observing that all their efforts, public and private, for the improvement of their civic conditions seemed to end in raising considerably
the rents of the ground landlords of London, while leaving the bulk
of the population engaged in a hard struggle for their existence,
that he had for years past found it difficult to take much interest
in municipal affairs, so long as the rates and taxes were—as it
seemed to him—put upon the wrong shoulders.   And for the study
of civics, he had preferred to turn to those cities where efforts were
being made to establish communal life on what seemed to him juster
conditions.   In 1897, he was struck with the title of an article in
the "Daily Telegraph."   It was headed, "The Land of Beauty,
Society without Poverty, Life without Care."   He found the article
was a description of Durban in Natal.   The writer attributed the
prosperity of this town to the fact that the suburbs were kept in
the hands of the community, instead of being handed over to private
owners who would absorb all the unearned increment.   Even if this
eulogium betrayed exaggeration still a student of civics might feel
that the economic conditions of that town were worth studying.
Similarly, in New Zealand, the adoption in 1891 of the tax on land
values brought prosperity to the towns, and changed the tide of
emigration from New Zealand into immigration.   Again, at home
they had Bourneville, Port Sunlight, and that most interesting of
all present-day experiments in this country, the Garden City, all of
these being founded by men with ideals.   He could not help feeling
|117| that a student of civics, possessed of such a fair working
knowledge of the city he lived in as most of them might reasonably
lay claim to, would make more real progress by studying the success
or failure of social experiments, than by entering on the very
formidable task that seemed to be set before them by Professor
Geddes.   However, when they left abstract civics, as they had it
portrayed to them in these papers, and turned to the architectural
or the historical side of concrete civics, there should be no better
guide than Professor Geddes, whose labours in Edinburgh, and
whose projected schemes for the improvement of Dunfermline, were
becoming widely known.

MR. TOMKINS (*of the London Trades Council*) said:
If before any person was allowed to serve on our different public

bodies, he should be required to attend a course of lectures such as those given by Professor Geddes on civics, that would surely be a means of developing his social interests, and would tend to eliminate that self-interest which too often actuated public men.   There was nothing more difficult than for workmen to-day to be able to take larger views.   The workman's whole business was now so different from what is was in the days of the arts and crafts guilds of the Middle Ages; they now found him ground down into some little division of industry, and it was quite impossible for him to work in his own way.   Thus he got narrow-minded, because concentrated on some minor process.   He was kept at work with his nose to the mill the whole time, and it became too exhausting for him to try and take these larger views of life.   He often thought of the amount of talent and energy and practical beauty which was wasted in our workshops to-day.   Referring to the Garden Cities of this country and the United States, Mr. Tomkins said the idea of getting great Trusts to use their money in a social spirit, and not merely to get the workers tied to their mills, was really something which opened out a vista of grand possibilities in the future; but if any movement was to be successful it would be necessary to teach the great masses of workers, and to create a real sound social public opinion amongst them.

PROFESSOR GEDDES' reply

Professor Geddes, in replying to the discussion, said he entirely agreed with the point made by Mr. Swinny, and he should just like to correct what he had said in his lecture by reference to what he meant by a civic museum.   In Edinburgh, he had in his museum a large room, with a geographical model |118| of the old town with its hill-fort, and so on; and he hung round this maps and diagrams of historical and geographical details.   On the opposite side of the room, he had a symbol of the market-cross, which stood for the centre of its municipal life, of its ideals and independence of environment.   Around it was grouped what represented the other side of the city; and here he might answer another point, and say that they could never settle the great philosophical controversy of determinism and free-will.   They would always incline when young to the novel of circumstance, and later, to the novel of character, but they should always feel that life was a game of individual skill with interfering circumstances. These diagrams of his were only the page split. On the one side, he meant to push to the extreme the idea that the place makes us, and on the other side, that we make the place. By what process do men struggle towards the selection of their ideals? They find themselves within the grasp of their environment, their whole heritage of culture, of good and ill, the whole tradition of the past; but they must select certain elements of these—the elements that seem to them good, and so they might escape from the manner of the city. Pointing to a drawing of the old Scotch bawbee, Professor Geddes said it was not a very dignified symbol of the coinage of the world, but let them mark how it had on the one side the hammerman at his work, with his motto "*Beat deus artem*," and, on the other side, a larger legend, with the eagle of the empire and the lamb of Saint John.

To return to his civic museum: the room below the one he had described was the larger museum for Scotland, and in the room below that, again, the museum for England, Ireland and America, the whole English-speaking world—not the Empire only. And the whole stood on a museum and library representing that larger evolution of the occidental civilisation which showed them they were merely children of the past. Professor Geddes pleaded for museums in which every city displayed its own past and present, but related itself to the whole of Europe and the whole occident.

One or two practical questions of great importance had |119| been raised; but, with all respect, he submitted that they could consider what was practical and practicable without requiring to go into the question of taxing land. That was a matter of political opinion. It was as if they were discussing the geology of coal, which they could do, without reference to coal royalties. Mr. Weymouth was with them on the subject of preserving old buildings; and he thought there was a great deal to be learned, if Mr. Weymouth would descend the valley of the Thames once more. It was of great importance if he found a great city at the tidal limit. Going down the Thames and the Tay, they would find, at the last ford of one, the old Abbey of Westminster, and at the last ford of the other, the old Abbey of Scoon. The kings of England and Scotland were crowned there because these were the most important places—a point of great historic interest. As a matter of practical interest, he might mention that Scoon and Westminster alike passed out of supreme importance when bridges were built across the river below; and he would next point out how just as Perth became of subordinate importance when the great Tay Bridge was built, so it became a tremendously important question to London, as it might in turn be much affected by the making of a great and a new bridge much further down the stream. This study of the descending river had real and practical, as well as historical importance.   He had been about considerably in the great cities of the United States, and had been struck by the amount of good endeavour there.   It was not, however, by denouncing Tammany that they could beat it, but by understanding it.   They must understand the mechanism by which the Celtic chieftain ruled his clan, and they must deal with these methods by still other methods; and they might often find it more satisfactory to re-moralise the chieftain than to destroy him.

Professor Geddes concluded by saying that he appreciated the admirable suggestion of Mr. Still towards the evolution of civic unions.   He was sure Mr. Still had there an idea of great significance which might be developed.